Wolves of Russia

Part Two:

The Long Walk

"For our freedom and yours."

(Dyslexia-friendly edition)

Published by Crossbridge Books
Worcester
www.crossbridgeeducational.com

ISBN 978 1 913946 24 1

British Library Cataloguing in Publication Data
A catalogue record for this book is available from the
British Library

CROSSBRIDGE
BOOKS

Wolves of Russia

Part Two:

The Long Walk

(Dyslexia-friendly edition)

R M Mace

'The wolf also shall dwell with the lamb,
The leopard shall lie down with the young goat,
The calf and the young lion and the fatling together,
And a little child shall lead them.
The cow and bear shall graze,
Their young ones shall lie down together,
And the lion shall eat straw like the ox.'

Isaiah 11:6-9

CONTENTS: Page:

Prologue to Part 2   1

Part 2 – The Long Walk

Chapter 10 – A privileged childhood (1939)   3

Chapter 11 – War and invasion (September 1939)   22

Chapter 12 – Excursion to Soviet Russia (October 1939) 34

Chapter 13 – Deportation (February 1940)   48

Chapter 14 – Siberia (1940)   59

Chapter 15 – Escape (March 1941)   82

Chapter 16 – Wolves (April 1941)   94

Chapter 17 – Alone (Spring 1941)   105

Chapter 18 – Captive again (Early Summer 1941)   117

Chapter 19 – A wedding (Mid-summer 1941)   134

Chapter 20 – The Kolkhoz (Late Summer 1941)   146

Chapter 21 – The Caspian Sea (Autumn 1941)   156

Historical note and copy of transcripts for Part Two   168

FOREWORD:

This book is based on the memoirs of a very dear friend of the family who gave his name as: Vincent Viktor Rudolf. Viktor's father died when he was just sixteen, so the early part of this story, told in Part One, though based on his recollections and true accounts, has been reconstructed using historical archives to fill in the 'missing gaps'.

Part Two tells Viktor's own story of deportation to Siberia, escape, and his long walk to Persia.

Viktor circa 1939

Viktor 2019

Dedicated to the dear memory of my mother,

Eileen Margaret Anne Mohr (1931-2022)

"Believe in God and He will be in your heart".

(Viktor November 2022)

PROLOGUE TO PART 2

"All I'm going to tell you now – I, Viktor, have lived in terrible times. Poland had been occupied by Russia many times – and Germany – one came from one side and the other came from the other side. And they found our land very useful, why? Because it is very good soil, and everybody wants it. So, from time to time there has been attack and separation. And when they separated Poland - that was in the king time - the Tsar. Then the communists came – very destructive, anything capitalist they kill.

After the war everything settled and returned back to normal, in Poland. Father was in engineering. Poland needed people like father, so father had a top job – as an architect; he was in charge of the rebuilding. Poland was just starting back on her feet. He was in the Polish free army under General Pilsudski. Poland after the first world war became free. Then we had our army – our everything – our Polish education – we were proud of our country.

In September 1939, when the communists came, my father was already in the army fighting Germans. This is my story."

PART TWO

THE LONG WALK

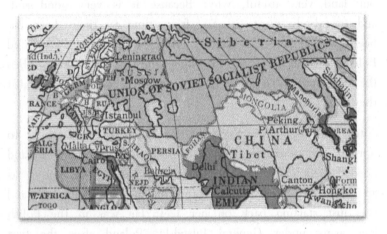

USSR before World War Two

CHAPTER 10

A PRIVILEGED CHILDHOOD (1939)

Lying amongst the plethora of flowering yellow rhododendron bushes, with the afternoon sun forcing its way between early leaves on the oak trees that stretched upwards, as if they were tall men wading through a saffron lake, the forest had a speckled sepia appearance. I lay motionless on my stomach, listening intently. Five of my school friends were also lying prone in the undergrowth listening. Whilst trekking in the nearby forest, we had spotted a very suspicious-looking man hiding amongst the bushes. Living so close to the Russian border, we knew it was our duty to track down and watch for Russian intruders who came over the border. We had followed strangers before and of course it always generated great excitement. We had kept our distance and been successfully watching the man's every movement without him knowing we were there. After several hours of surveillance, I decided that the time had come to report him to the authorities and gestured to Tadeusz, who was nearest to me to come closer.

We both raised ourselves slowly onto hands and knees and cautiously moved toward each other. Wincing, but managing to stifle the expletive that rose to my lips as a sharp twig dug into my wrist, I crawled close enough to speak directly into Tadeusz's ear.

"We've been watching him for hours," I whispered, "one of us needs to report this to the police," I continued in a tone that did not expect opposition.

"Let me go, I'm as quick as anyone else," came the breathless reply, "but don't let him out of your sight."

After a quick glance round at the others, who seemed instinctively to know what we had decided, I nodded my approval and lowered myself back down onto the soft grassy soil as Tadeusz edged away, endeavouring as he did so to create as little disturbance as possible, before setting off towards Rovno town. I hoped he would find someone willing to come back with him when he got there.

I felt something crawling along my hand and looked down to see a small trickle of blood from the cut on my wrist and made a mental note to give it a good clean at the earliest opportunity. Just in front of me, I could see Anton lift himself up and draw his legs up into a crouching position so that he could look over the top of some dark foliage. Anton was the only one of us who had a pair of binoculars with him; I wished I had mine. If we could see what the man was up to, we would have a better idea of how dangerous he might be. A starving Russian peasant would be a lot easier to handle than a fully trained spy. Moments later Anton was crouching down again and frantically waving at me to move closer. Scanning the ground for dry twigs to avoid, I edged forward.

"He's moving; quick, we need to get closer; we mustn't lose sight of him now," hissed Anton.

"Keep down you idiot," I mouthed back at him, hardly daring to make even the smallest sound, "Just keep an eye on him from here."

"If he gets away, we'll have wasted a whole day," muttered Anton moodily, lowering himself back down into the shadows. Of course, I felt the same way, but one thing that had been drilled into us in our scout training was the value of patience and timing. The other three boys were spread out some distance away and I began to get worried that they might break cover if they didn't get some kind of communication from us soon. I indicated to Anton to stay where he was while I tried to get to Jerzy who happened to be nearest to us.

There wasn't much ground cover between me and Jerzy, so I scooped up some mud and rubbed it over my face and hands to give me some camouflage in the sun-flecked undergrowth between the trees. Anton evidently thought this was unnecessary and shook his head doubtfully. I thought about attracting Jerzy's attention by lobbing a small pebble at him but decided it was too risky. Instead, walking on hands and feet, and moving sideways like a crab so that I could keep an eye on our prey, I sidled slowly across to where Jerzy was lying barely visible under the rhododendron bushes. He nearly jumped out of his skin when my darkened face appeared above him and clamped his own hand over his mouth. His eyes, at first widened with fear, began to crinkle with laughter as he recognised me under my muddy mask. I indicated that he should stay down and keep quiet.

Meanwhile, unbeknownst to the rest of us, Leon, who happened also to be the youngest, was still moving steadily closer to our suspect, curiosity drawing him ever nearer. Suddenly we heard a rustle of bushes, a yelp, and a sharp male voice expletive from the direction of the suspicious-looking man. Almost immediately, Anton appeared at my side and together we raised our heads above our parapet to try to see what was happening. To our utter horror, we could see that the man had caught hold of Leon in what looked like an iron grip. We heard him speak in well-educated Polish,

"Why are you here and what are you doing?"

"Just going for a walk in the forest," answered Leon, his voice betraying a tremor. At this point I became aware that I had stopped breathing and took a gulp of air. I had no idea what the others were doing as my eyes were riveted to the scene unfolding in front of me. Adrenalin was surging through my veins, and I felt ready to explode. Moments later I saw the man take out a knife with one hand and lift Leon's chin with the other; I had no doubt of his intentions. A terrible rage took hold of me, and without thinking, I charged forward with a strange roar and launched myself at the man. As I reached for my own scout knife, I became aware that the others had sprung forward with me like a pack of hungry wolves. Fortunately for us, he was taken by surprise. I had taken hold of the arm that was wielding the knife while Anton had grabbed the other arm and managed to pin it behind him. Meanwhile Jerzy and Pawel, arriving just seconds after us, had kicked his legs from under him. We managed to roll him onto his front with his arms pinned behind him having disarmed him. It took four of us to sit on him, Leon and Pawel sat on a leg each whilst the rest of us took it in turns to sit on his back while one person kept a look out for the police.

Our prisoner didn't speak a word; he just lay quietly, occasionally lifting his head slightly to spit the dust from his mouth. Anton kept trying to ask him questions and began to get annoyed when he didn't get an answer.

"He doesn't seem like a Russian peasant to me," Anton had growled, "because he spoke good Polish; that means he must be a dirty Russian spy. You ask him something Viktor; you're the only one here who speaks Russian."

"If he is a spy, he won't answer whatever language I use," I said, wondering how long the police would take to arrive because we had all been out for hours and were getting hungry and fed up with sitting on the man.

Eventually, Jerzy, who was on lookout, started waving and jumping up and down calling out,

"Over here; we've captured a prisoner; it's a Russian spy!"

Much to our relief, three policemen had followed Tadeusz into the forest, probably out of curiosity. They quickly assessed the situation and arrested the man, confiscating all his belongings, and hauling him away. Tadeusz wanted to know what had happened and was disappointed to have missed all the action.

We found out later that the man was German but spoke perfect Polish and Russian and turned out to be a secret agent. Because we had been the ones to discover and capture him, we were allowed to help the border guards (the KOP), and the police to search for evidence in the forest. After about two days, all his belongings were discovered. There were all sorts of sabotage equipment, changes of clothes for disguising himself, bedding, and even iron-ration tablets. We were never told the whole story, but for our patriotic work, the authorities acknowledged their gratitude and gave our school a radio in appreciation.

My mother wasn't keen on our exploits in the forest but perfectly understood the importance of helping to keep our borders safe. My younger sister Anna listened with shining eyes as I described our capture of the German agent.

"But why are the Germans spying on us?" she wondered, "I thought it was just the Russians." With the superiority of an elder brother, I paraphrased the oft-repeated words of our father on the subject.

"There are Germans infiltrating the German colonies in the area, you know like the one where Grandmother is from…"

"Grandmother is not a spy!" declared Anna indignantly.

"Of course not, but there are a lot of Germans in Rovno district and they're not all friendly to the Republic. Well Father says that they have been supplying guns and ammunition and spreading rumours to stir up trouble."

Mother scowled at me, and I knew that she would rather I changed the subject, so I kept my further thoughts to myself. I had overheard my father speaking with some of his friends about the increasing number of German spies and fifth columnists being sent into Poland. He believed that they were secretly training Ukrainian nationalists living in Poland and forming elite military units to help with a future German invasion.

As we lived so close to the border with the Russians, or perhaps I should say the Ukrainian Soviet Socialist Republic, older schoolboys, Air Force Cadets, Boy Scouts, and other civilian organisations were given the task of helping to track down and watch for Russian intruders who came over the border in hordes. Despite a strong Border Guard, we knew that intruders and saboteurs continually entered Poland to try to destabilise the country. The police and Border Guards couldn't arrest everyone who came over and so we boys were used as a third line of defence in reporting suspicious-looking people to the authorities. I had often heard my parents discussing the intruders, who usually lived rough in the forests and made for small villages where they had contacts and were then able to send reports back to Russia about our newly built military installations, river bridges, and railway lines.

The forests around the town had become quite dangerous because of the number of people crossing illegally from Russia. As well as criminals and spies, every day, crowds of ordinary Russians tried to escape to Poland from the communist regime, mostly because they were desperately short of food. They had great difficulty in crossing the border because the Russian guards had instructions to shoot to kill any of their citizens who tried escaping into Poland. Those refugees that did make it across the border told stories of terrible living conditions, of food being requisitioned by the Soviet authorities and of deportations to Siberia. It was rumoured that Russian people who lived in villages on the border were not even allowed to look across into Poland, and no Polish persons were allowed to enter Russia for any reason. According to my Father, the Polish government had informed the League of Nations, but Russia always denied the situation and said it was Polish propaganda against the Communist regime.

But despite the fragile existence of our Polish Republic, my sister and I had a privileged and enviable childhood. We lived in a large, three-storey house that was thought to be over three-hundred years old. I had my own playroom, and we had a nanny. At the top of the house was an attic that was full of old furniture, ladies' crinolines from the previous century, and old paintings. There was also a collection of ancient weapons, so we were banned from visiting the attic by ourselves. The house was near the station, on the west side of town. The military barracks for the cavalry garrison, and a small military aerodrome were also nearby.

From the age of four, Anna and I were taught to ski, skate, and ride, as well as other sports. I must admit that I preferred riding my bicycle to riding a horse. Father taught me to play the violin, but I didn't learn to play the piano like Mother or Grandmother. We didn't own a car, but Father had the use of a government car and a chauffeur who would collect and drive us where we needed to go. We had everything we wanted. My hand-made shirts were silk, and all our shoes were hand made. We were given pocket money to spend; I never seemed to have enough for all my hobbies.

To me it seemed that we lived in a beautiful small town where there was always something interesting to see and do. I remember that there was a real mix of religions, Catholic, Orthodox, Jews and Lutherans, who as far as I was aware all lived together in harmony; it was forbidden for anyone to denigrate another religion or nationality. We were all supposed to be citizen of the Polish Republic regardless of creed. On Sundays, the military band would march through the town and into our church to take part in the Mass. We had a very big choir – there were hundreds of them, and with the military band there was always a wonderful rendition of the hymns that was often so loud that the roof and windows of the church would rattle.

In the autumn, the army would return to barracks after a few months of manoeuvres and it would take hours for at least ten thousand men, horses, and tanks, as well as heavy artillery, to march through the town. My sister wasn't really interested, so I would meet up with some of my friends to join in with the townsfolk who came out to meet them with flowers and sweets to welcome them back. Families along the route of the march decorated their houses with flags and flowers. For me these parades were like carnivals where all the people were happy, friendly, and respectful towards the military. At Christmas and Easter, the army held parties and invited the townsfolk, and at the weekend the band played in the local parks and arranged firework displays.

"And they do more than just parade about," I remember saying to Anna when she pulled a face about going to see a parade, "They help the children from the orphanage, and as you very well know, children from the elementary school can go to the barracks for the leftovers after school if they're hungry," I said proudly, having heard Mother telling a neighbour about what happened to the leftovers from the army kitchens. She had also told the neighbour that when a family she knew needed help, they went to the military commandant at the garrison who said he was happy to give assistance including food and clothing.

One of my favourite annual events was the provincial fair that was held in our town every September. In 1936, the newspapers reported that there were ninety-six thousand visitors that year; I think that was the biggest, although I can't imagine how they counted them. Exhibitors came from all over Poland, bringing with them engineering products, fabrics, chemicals, building materials, and novelties to show and sell. Even my sister enjoyed these fairs, and we spent many happy hours collecting free samples, picking up free literature, and watching demonstrations. At the same time there was always a large circus that came to town with the fair that caused great excitement and was where much of our pocket money was spent. At the last fair that I went to I was old enough to be able to stay out until dark to listen to the different bands that played in the park in the evenings and watch some of the dancing. All the shops around the exhibition stayed open all night, as did the restaurants in the centre of town, to cater for the visitors. People came from Hungary, Romania, Czechoslovakia, and other neighbouring countries, except Russia — they weren't allowed to leave their country.

On warm summer evenings, there were gypsy bands to entertain us with their dancing and singing. They would build fires in the clearings in the woods, and invite townsfolk, and residents of the military settlements, out for an evening of musical entertainment; they always made a collection afterwards. Those warm summer nights with the sound of the gypsy pipes and fiddles mingled with the crackling of the fires and the smell of the smoky air, and the fluttering of coloured ribbons made us feel as though we could simply live our whole lives in the forest amongst the lush vegetation and wildlife and live off nuts and berries as our ancient forbears must have done. There were also small parish fairs in the nearby villages where we could buy things like cap guns, clay or tin whistles or even trumpets.

My father had been brought up in a very different world from the one that my sister and I found ourselves in. He had been a Count, the son of a Count, and heir to a great estate. But for the Bolsheviks, as the next in line, I would have inherited the title and the estate. The military discipline and social etiquette of the Imperial Court were firmly embedded in my father's way of life and we children were expected to behave accordingly. Discipline was very strict in our household compared to the families of our friends and acquaintance as was the insistence on politeness; I was always expected to kiss my mother's hand, and when guests came, we knew our place.

Because of Father's role in government, and with him being a reserve officer, I went to a special boarding school. It was a military school for the sons of officers, paid for by the government, in preparation for a military career. We had to learn languages and to this day I speak fluent Russian and German as well as Polish my mother tongue. When I was twelve, I transferred to a private school in Rovno where I learned to shoot and had further general preparation for life in the services. We were taught leadership skills, fencing, and communication skills. But I learned to jump with a parachute from a tower in the Air Force cadets. We spent a great deal of time orienteering and living off the land and also had to spend many nights finding our way through the forest with only a compass, torch and maps – this training was to save my life later on.

As children, we rarely saw Father as he worked away from home six days a week and we were only together on Sundays. He had great respect for Marshal Pilsudski and must have known him well because I remember, before he died in 1935, playing with his daughters Wanda and Jadwiga when we visited them at the Belvedere palace in Warsaw. Jadwiga, the younger sister, was only a few years older than me; she built model aeroplanes. We knew Father was involved in secret government work, and as we lived close to the Russian border, he needed protection from their secret agents and had a permanent bodyguard. At home, we had a specially trained Alsatian guard dog to watch out for intruders. Father was also Chairman of one of the banks and that kept him even busier. So, for us, Sunday was always a wonderful day, since it was the only day Father spent with us at home.

We children were on our best behaviour and tried to please him and make it a happy family day; yet we were also slightly afraid of him because his expectations and standards of behaviour were so high. On some occasions, I used to serve as an altar boy at Mass.

We had two ways of life at home. Monday to Saturday with Mother was relaxed and casual, and Saturday evening, when Father arrived home until early Monday morning when he left for the office, were always very formal, with good behaviour expected. When Father arrived on Saturday evening, he always brought us children a large bag of sweets and chocolates and a present for Mother. I think this was his way of saying sorry for not being with us during the week. On Sunday mornings, Father would question us closely on our progress at school and what we had been doing with ourselves during the week. Then he would look through our homework books and ask us to read for him from our schoolbooks. Anna was very clever and seemed to be able to remember everything after reading it just once. I have to admit that I was envious of her; learning something seemed to be much harder work for me. After either his approval or disapproval of our work, Father told us what he expected from us the following week. When he had time, he would tell us fairy stories, for which he had a real gift, and we were very happy just to sit with him. I always followed him around like a loyal little puppy and could not bear to part with him on Monday mornings.

Often on Sundays there wasn't time to go to church, so we had our own family prayers in the house. We had a small altar with a crucifix and our own prayer books.

Father would read and say a prayer, and then we sang a hymn, which I never enjoyed; I preferred the Mass in church. Afterwards, there would be a programme arranged for the rest of the day. If the weather was fine, we sometimes went to a restaurant for lunch and then a walk in the park or the forest in the afternoon, or we went boating on the river Horyn. We often went riding in the forest together; Father, as a reserve cavalry officer, loved to ride. The stables would deliver four horses to the house at about two o'clock and we would spend the afternoon riding. In the woodland we might come across fields of violets and tiny streams with crystal clear water and tiny green frogs. After our ride, we either took the horses back to the stables or they were collected from home by the stable hands. In winter, we regularly went skiing, which I had learnt from the age of four and had become quite proficient. The whole family enjoyed outdoor activities.

We had a very full social life. Mother invited lots of friends to visit us in the week whilst Father was away at the office. During the hot weather we had barbeques and garden parties for our family and school friends. Our own garden was very productive, with a good variety of fruit and vegetables. We had one enormous pear tree with so much fruit that we, even all our family and friends, could not eat it all, so Mother sold almost the entire crop to local merchants who picked and packed them and sold them in their stores. If Father was home when we had our family gatherings, there would be singing and dancing — which Father adored, or his friends brought their musical instruments to the house, and we had a musical evening with Father playing the violin and Mother playing the piano.

The river Horyn was not far away, and we spent many of our summer days swimming, sailing and fishing. The fish were very plentiful and varied so this was a popular pastime. On our side of the river, the land was low-lying meadow covered with marigolds, hedged with blossoming bird cherry and at the river's edge with sweet rushes. The opposite bank, across the dark wide river where it was fast-flowing and winding, was high and steep and we would often see the children from the military settlements sliding down to the river's edge. The river was in beautiful surroundings, overgrown with willow trees and with masses of different birds. On the far bank were old orchards and lilac bushes. The bridge that used to span the river had been burnt down during the wars in which my father had fought and the local military settlers, who lived on the other side of the river, had set up a ferry crossing. In the summer holidays, students from Warsaw flocked into the area to stay in tents, bringing their canoes with them. The students taught the local children how to swim and play volleyball. They dug out the ground to make tables covered with fronds of bracken for their picnic banquets. The local scouts would join in with field exercises and campfires, and they would head off into the forest to pick wild strawberries, nuts and mushrooms or join in swimming or fishing in the river. To commemorate May 3rd (Constitution Day - to celebrate the declaration of the Constitution in 1791), school children would gather near the river to sing songs, dance national dances and recite poems. They would build rafts, boats and kayaks and organise races. In the evening, by moonlight and the light of the bonfires, they would make wreaths out of flowers and float them on the river. There were also Church fairs when people would celebrate the patron saint of the local church on their feast days. There would be plenty of food and stalls of sweets and crafts.

Father believed that the reason the region where we lived had been invaded so often was because it was so fertile. The soil around us was very rich, and the markets were bursting with fruit and vegetables. I remember once fetching a bucket of cherries for preserving for what would be about 4p – it was hardly worth the farmers picking them. We had such warm summers that tomatoes grew outside, and no one ever needed a greenhouse. We picked mushrooms from the forest and dried them for winter soups. We also picked wild strawberries and bilberries. If you were poor, there was plenty of food available just for the picking. Local farmers grew hops, sweetcorn, buckwheat and rye that would grow taller than a man. But it was the orchards that the region was famous for with a huge variety of apples and cherries.

Fruit trees were something my maternal grandfather, Józef, knew all about. After he had retired from the army, he had spent many months travelling all over Europe, including France, Italy, and Holland, collecting unusual varieties of apples, pear, and plums. He had a large house built amongst his orchards. He became such an expert on the propagation of fruit trees and the introduction of different varieties that he wrote a book on the subject. My grandmother was forty years younger than him when they were married, and she had to report to him every week on the household supplies and account for every zloty she had spent. In the orchards he kept about two-hundred beehives and we always had plenty of honey, and grandmother would sell most of it. Grandfather had a special room for drying apples, pears, and plums. He grew the largest pears I have ever seen anywhere, with juice like honey. He rarely visited us in Rovno and when he did, he only stayed for a few hours. He didn't like town and only lived for his bees and his fruit trees.

Mother, Anna, and I visited him frequently, usually while Father was away at work, and I loved the time I spent with him in the orchards. He was a deeply religious person; he did not drink socially, but following his old army custom, every morning before breakfast, he had one tot of pure spirits or vodka, which he firmly believed kept him healthy. Perhaps it was the reason for his good health since he had not visited a doctor since having his medical examination when he joined the army as a young man.

In the May of 1939, we paid one of our visits to my grandparents. Grandfather took me outside with him when he went out to check on his bees.

"The weather has been so dry that my poor bees have not been able to collect the nectar from the pollen," he told me sadly. "They have been collecting the nectar from somewhere else to feed the larvae who have eaten it all, so I don't think we will have much honey at all this year," he added as his gaze lingered somewhere on the horizon, and then his thoughts seemed to drift away. Grandmother had warned us that it wasn't safe to let him walk alone in case he fell, and I could feel him leaning heavily against me.

"I expect there will be plenty of fruit," I said hoping to cheer him up. He sighed, lifted his head, and again seemed to look a long way into the distance as if expecting to see something emerge over the horizon.

"It's been so dry," he said again, clearly fixed on this thought. He looked a little pale and I was worried that he might be getting cold.

"Are you warm enough?" I asked cautiously, not wanting to offend the brave old warrior, "Shall I fetch a shawl?" He smiled and nodded at me. I led him near to a tree to lean against whilst I ran into the house to fetch a shawl. Grandmother fussed about which shawl would be best and, in the end, came out with me carrying several different warm garments. We found him lying on the ground under one of his favourite trees, looking as if he had fallen asleep. But when we tried to rouse him, we discovered that he had peacefully passed away. He was a hundred-and-five.

In their home, my grandparents had a large oil painting of grandfather, uniformed with a long spike on top of his helmet, holding his sword and sitting on horseback. He had been a cavalry captain in the former Austrian Army, but this was not something that people in the new Polish Republic would want to be reminded of, so the painting had been relegated to the attic. The silver sword that he was brandishing in the painting was left to me in his will along with a very expensive revolver that was to be given to me when I was older. As the only male heir, I was also to inherit the house and orchards on grandmother's death.

I was very proud of the sword which I was allowed to take home so that I could use it to practise my fencing. Jumping on the bed and showing off to Anna, I imagined myself as a swashbuckling buccaneer and idiotically waved the sword around without proper care.

"En garde!" I yelled and swung the sword low. As I bounced on the bed, I misjudged the distance and the sharp blade sliced through my shoe and badly cut my toes. I still have the scar to this day.

CHAPTER 11

WAR AND INVASION (SEPTEMBER 1939)

We had a beautiful dry summer in 1939. During the heat of the day Mother withdrew into the cool of the house, sat down at her grand piano and filled the air with the music of Chopin. But we could sense her disquiet. There was an unfamiliar stillness that hung in the air even in the bustling town. The trees in the parks, forests and woodland were already turning gold and red with their early autumnal colours. Father came home and many of his friends gathered in our house to discuss their fears of the possibility of an approaching war. It seemed that the German army was accumulating armaments and talking of expansion toward the east.

"Poland has only limited funds to spend on armaments, and we have not had enough time to build up sufficient industry to produce the arms needed to defend ourselves," Father warned. I was allowed to listen in at these meetings since it was our future that was at stake, and Father considered me old enough to understand what was happening.

"The government have tried to look for ways to avoid trouble with Germany, but it's proving impossible," said one of the men present, "and I don't trust the Bolsheviks' promise not to attack us in the east," he added darkly.

"After just twenty years of freedom and independence, it looks as if we are in trouble again; we can only hope for a miracle to happen to save us," Father had said despondently.

"England, France, and America say they will support us against Germany," said one member of the group, trying to sound positive.

"Yes, but Britain has forbidden us to mobilise our forces because they say that this would inflame the Germans into taking action, because then they could say that we had started it by mobilising," added my father, effectively putting a damper on any hopes of outside support. We knew the war was close. Before I went on my summer holiday, Father, as were many others, was recalled to the army, with the rank of Colonel. This was done as discreetly as possible so that our enemies would be unaware of our actions. As he left, Father took me aside.

"You are the man of the house while I am away, and it is your responsibility to look after your mother and sister. You must defend them and find food for them if it becomes necessary," he said gravely. Then he silently gave me his revolver. Just as he was leaving, he turned and made one final request.

"Bury all the family silver and other valuables in the garden," then with a twisted smile added,

"That includes grandfathers' sword." He ran down the steps and climbed into the waiting car without looking back. Mother appeared at my side, and putting an arm around my shoulder, and speaking softly but with a fierceness in her voice told me,

"Remember it is your duty to fight and give your life, if necessary, for your country because you have never lost your freedom and you do not know what it means to be occupied by a foreign power."

I went for my summer holiday in August with the Boy Scouts and during this holiday we spent a lot of time preparing for the anticipated war. Every day we had political discussions, training in sabotage, how to use different weapons and explosives, throwing dummy grenades, and learning to recognise the uniforms and ranks of different sections of the German army. We were all trained to use various types of equipment in case we would be needed to help with an underground army. Being boys, we were very keen, and I think many of us even looked forward to any forthcoming trouble.

The weather was still beautiful in the autumn that year, but the day I returned home for the beginning of the school term, during the night of September 1st, the German army invaded Poland. In the morning, Mother came and found me; she was as white as a ghost, she said,

"I have just heard on the wireless... the Germans invaded Poland in the early hours of this morning."

School was immediately suspended, and all able-bodied civilians were directed to help with the preparations to defend the town. A few days later, new conscripts began arriving on the outskirts of town to guard the bridges and viaducts while the rest of the army, including our Rovno Garrison, was already engaged in fighting on the western front to defend Warsaw. General mobilisation had still not taken place because Poland had been trying to avoid giving Germany any excuse for attacking us.

German bombers attacked our local railway station and the surrounding town, destroying a lot of military equipment. By the second week there were huge crowds of civilians – refugees fleeing east from the German front, mostly coming up from the direction of Brody. They had all their possessions with them, including small babies in prams. We heard stories that in the evenings the German planes had started shooting the crowds with machine guns. People had nowhere to hide because there were only fields on both sides of the road. According to radio reports, German fighter aircraft were even firing on young shepherd boys in the fields.

During the day we dug trenches to protect ourselves against further air attacks and I remember seeing grown men crying in frustration because they could not enlist. It was rumoured that many brave men had volunteered for suicide missions – strapping explosives around their bodies to destroy enemy tanks. Meanwhile, the civilian authorities began to organise help for the hospitals and for the families of those who would be joining the army. Food was stored in places that would be safe from destruction, and large amounts of money was collected from the public as a contribution to the war effort.

Then, very early in the morning of September 17th, while we in the eastern borderlands were utterly defenceless, hundreds of Russian planes began to bomb the roads, railway lines, and river bridges. Following in their wake, endless columns of tanks rolled across the Polish border, with hordes of troops, cavalry, and artillery advancing towards us without any declaration of war. They must have been gathering for weeks, and the invasion had clearly been planned long before the German invasion in the west of the country.

As the first tanks approached the town, the Russian soldiers could be heard telling us that they had come to help fight the Germans so we should not oppose them because they were our friends. One man called out to them,

"What have you brought for the people?"

"It's your day!" came the chilling reply, "It's time for the bloodsuckers to go."

In the evenings, when Anna was safely in bed, Mother and I would discuss our situation, carefully avoiding talk about Father who we knew was engaged in battle somewhere on the western front.

"I don't see how we can defend ourselves fighting on two fronts," she said, "and the border with Russia is so long; it stretches from Lithuania to Romania. To defend our eastern border, we would need the entire army," she added despondently.

"Our cavalry officers are world famous for their bravery," I reminded her, but I knew as well as she did, they would be unable to prevail against tanks.

"Your father anticipated some of this and there are already plans for an underground army, in fact an underground military organisation has existed for many years, but it will need the utmost and absolute secrecy," Mother had confided, "and if you Boy Scouts organise your own resistance you must tell no one, not Anna, and not even me — to protect all of us," she continued. I was very surprised; I had not imagined that Mother would involve herself in any underground army. But she was right; very soon the Scouts started to organise their own resistance.

In a short while, the Russian army had occupied the eastern parts of Poland as far as the river Bug, with the German army occupying the rest of the country to the west of the river, as had been agreed between Stalin and Hitler. We found ourselves surprised at how poorly equipped and badly maintained their army was. It was only their sheer numbers, and the fact that our army had been diverted, that had enabled them to overcome us. Our district was captured by the Ukrainian Front who were operating alongside the Red Army. They had orders immediately to arrest all military officers, police officers, gendarmes, intelligence and counter-intelligence officers, officials, and representatives of the political and economic elites, landed aristocracy, and military settlers and foresters. They were also to root out groups and persons intent on subversion, insurgent activity, or sabotage; they were to dispose of persons who were classed as hostile or socially dangerous.

We Boy Scouts were determined to create as much havoc as possible. We were organised into groups of five scouts, ages ranging from twelve to seventeen. We were supposed to cooperate with other units but were only to know each other by our assumed names; I was known as

Teddy. We also included girls in the groups; they were invaluable and extremely brave.

Our group decided to meet in the basement of a house in one of the narrow back streets of the town. We each had instructions to arrive from different directions and make absolutely sure that we were not followed, by taking devious routes, back tracking, and pretending to go into shops. We introduced ourselves using our nom de guerre and waited to see who would be in charge of the group. A Scout who was a few years older than me introduced himself as Rogue and told us that it would be his role to delegate tasks to the rest of us. He was tall and fresh faced; there was nothing roguish about him, but there was an intense fervour and passion in his voice. In the sparsely furnished room, there were piles of leaflets calling on the people of Poland to unite and fight for the restoration of the Polish Republic.

"The first thing we have to do, before anything else, is for us all to swear a sacred oath of loyalty and allegiance to the Republic and each other," Rogue told us. We all agreed to do this and then someone suggested that we put in writing our commitment and vows to the group.

"Won't that mean that there will be dangerous evidence of what we are doing; suppose a spy or a collaborator finds them?" I asked, hoping that it didn't make me sound cowardly.

"I've thought of that," said Rogue, "but if we are all using our nom de guerre, they won't have a clue who we are." I was glad that he had already thought of that, so I didn't look foolish.

"So, what sort of things will we be doing?" asked a girl who was probably close in age to Rogue and had introduced herself as Fairy.

"We have three main objectives," replied Rogue, "combat, intelligence collection, and informing." He went on to explain that our aim was to collect statistical data on the Red Army and the movements of their units, that we would be expected to carry out acts of sabotage, disseminate leaflets like the ones I had seen, enlist new members, collect weapons, and maintain contact with the underground army. "We need to put together a plan of action, who's doing what and so on," he said looking around to see if anyone would volunteer some ideas, while he poured out some glasses of water.

We agreed to meet up again in the next few days and bring our ideas to draft a plan and decide how we would keep some sort of record as reports to pass on to the underground army. At the next meeting, we made plans to blow up railway lines, rob food from trains, and distribute food to the elderly civilians in the town. One of the older boys wanted to carry out assassinations by buying poison.

"We can put a note on the bodies of killed Bolsheviks saying, 'Tell Saint Peter that you are not the first, and not the last'," he added with chilling humour.

But our group mainly stuck to stealing from the Russians by various tricks. The young Russian soldiers were so green and nervous that it was quite easy to hoodwink them. Eventually, with the help of stolen uniforms, we were able to get practically anywhere amongst them, and stole rifles, grenades, and other equipment. One of our favourite forms of attack was to throw a grenade into one of their tanks. We were not always successful and some of our Scouts were executed on the spot when they were found out; Rogue was arrested in the December and executed. The invading army had no mercy at all with anyone found in the wrong place at the wrong time.

On one occasion, Fairy and some other girls came up with a plan to entice two Russian officers to a party. The rest of the group arranged for there to be plenty of vodka, some gypsy music played on somebody's fiddle, and dancing. The Russian officers needed very little persuasion to join the party lured by the vodka. We all pretended to be drinking with them, saying how the dancing was making us thirsty. It wasn't long before they were both totally drunk. Fairy stood looking over them in disgust.

"Teddy, help me to strip them of their uniforms," she said, "I'm sure they will be really useful for the intelligence work of our underground army. Make sure you are careful with the fastenings; we don't want to tear the cloth or leave any marks," she added with foresight.

"What about their weapons?" I asked hoping for a keepsake.

"If you are caught with a weapon, you will be shot," she stated in a matter-of-fact voice, "The weapons will go to the army with the uniforms."

We dragged the semi-conscious soldiers out into an alley, leaving them in their soiled and sodden underclothes. What must have happened to the poor fellows when they returned to their unit I can only guess. This was all happening during the early days of the occupation. Later, the Russians having found that the population was not cooperating with them, became more alert to our schemes. The soldiers, knowing they could no longer walk safely on their own in town, kept in groups of three or four.

As the Russian troops consolidated their position, they started systematically to strip the shops, factories, and private houses of whatever it was possible to move, and they loaded them into trains to be transported to Russia. The ordinary soldiers could not believe that we lived in such comfort. Their troops had very little to eat and requisitioned food from the townspeople and local villages. Under cover of dark, groups of hungry Russian soldiers attacked farms, taking away anything edible, either dead or alive. Their staple army food seemed to be a porridge made from rye, and black bread. It was clearly inadequate; evidently the mighty Russian army could not feed their own soldiers, and although they were our enemy, we felt sorry for them.

We were astonished to see their uniforms in rags and tatters even though the war had only just begun. Many of the soldiers carried their rifles on a piece of string instead of a leather strap. Their shoes were never cleaned; they were covered with some sort of foul-smelling liquid to preserve them from wet weather. We couldn't bear to stand anywhere near them, and their poor level of hygiene exacerbated the situation. We Scouts began to make jokes about the mighty Russian army, and we even heard Russian soldiers themselves admitting that they had good technology but no culture.

It was not long before the Russian soldiers came to our house in search of loot. They arrived in front of the house, demanding entry, pushing their way unceremoniously past our nanny and lumbering into the drawing room where Mother had just been playing on her piano.

"Surrender your weapons!" ordered one of the men in Russian. Mother nodded at me, and I reluctantly went and fetched the one revolver that Father had given me before he left for our protection. It wouldn't have done any good to have refused; they would doubtless have torn the house apart with enthusiasm on the pretext of looking for illegal weapons.

"Assemble all the inhabitants of the house," came the next order. Mother looked visibly shaken by this but nevertheless called Anna, our nanny and the cook into the hallway where we assembled.

"Outside, capitalist bloodsuckers!" The next order was barked out and we found ourselves being escorted out of the house and into the road at gun point. A couple of soldiers stood behind us with guns pointed at us while several of the others went back into the house and began their looting. I remember the nerves on my back tingling in anticipation of a bullet that might hit me there. Mother had her arms protectively around Anna who was sobbing silently. But they were not interested in executions at this time; only looting. From our house they took blankets, clothes, cooking utensils and small pieces of furniture.

Mother had stayed completely calm at first, then, as a stricken look came over her face, we watched with a kind of horrified awe as the soldiers emerged from the doorway with Mother's beautiful grand piano. They had evidently already removed the legs and stood it on its side and were dragging it on a rug out towards where a cart had been brought to transport all our dearest moveable things to Russia, where it would no doubt be chopped up for firewood. I can only imagine how hard it must have been for Mother to watch that beautiful instrument — the source of her solace when Father was away, being taken away by those robbers.

"But we are all unharmed, and even grand pianos can be replaced," she had told us and then had said no more on the subject.

CHAPTER 12

EXCURSION INTO SOVIET RUSSIA (OCTOBER 1939)

After Poland capitulated, Father still did not return home. From what Mother didn't say, I guessed that he had gone underground with the rest of the surviving Polish army. I was sure that Mother was still secretly in contact with him; she went for long walks alone in the forest. I didn't ask questions; I knew that we were all safer the less anyone knew about the goings on of the underground army. There were spies and traitors everywhere; the NKVD (later known as KGB) were expert at interrogation.

In early October, I decided to go into Russia to visit Father's cousin Joseph. I had never seen him, but I knew that he lived in a town called Zaslaw, about thirty miles away. The last contact between the families had been in 1922 for my parent's wedding. Now that we were under Russian occupation, I wanted to let them know where we lived in case they ever came into Russian-occupied Poland. All I knew was his name and roughly where he lived; I didn't know the exact address.

It took me five days to get to Zaslaw because although Poland was now occupied by the Red Army, they still guarded the border with special troops and dogs. In many places the fences were protected by electric wires, although this was intended to keep their own people inside Russia.

I knew how difficult it was going to be but decided to risk it and go.

My biggest problem was actually crossing the border. I spent a whole day hiding in the bushes and watching the guards. I could see that the land around had been carefully ploughed and several times during the day the bare earth was raked over so that any footprints would be immediately visible. I needed to plot a route so that I could scramble from one bush to another without leaving any footprints. What made it trickier was that the guards, as well as inspecting the ground for footprints, searched around the bushes, using their rifles to push back the branches. Where they chose to search seemed to be random rather than systematic; that made it much harder to predict which bushes might be safe to use. Eventually I decided on a route that took me across the danger zone in the shortest possible time and took the plunge.

Crouching behind bushes was something that I had become very adept at in our own woods and forests, and, although I slipped several times on wet leaves, I didn't lose my footing. About two-thirds of the way across, one of the guards changed direction so that he was only about five metres away from me; my heart sank with fright, and I held my breath wondering if I would make it back the way I had come without being shot at if I had to run for it. My luck held when he turned and moved away in the other direction. I jumped across to the bush that he had previously been searching around on the assumption that he wouldn't be likely to go that way again straight away. Eventually I made it safely across.

Walking only at night, I made my way south to Zaslaw. My next problem was how to find my family. The small town lay right on the river Horyn. The single-storey houses, that appeared to have been built haphazardly rather than along main thoroughfares, had white-washed walls and shuttered windows. A couple of church buildings rose above the rest, and on a higher level above the river were some much bigger buildings that looked as if they could be houses of former nobility and probably now occupied by Soviet officials. There were also some tall buildings that looked as if they had been built in the middle of the river, on small islands. The town was swarming with troops. There were easily recognised members of the NKVD, wearing their distinctive peak caps of light blue with a carmine red stripe, on the lookout for suspicious-looking people, checking the internal passports of anyone they suspected. In those days it was necessary to have an internal passport to travel from one town to another.

Trying to walk nonchalantly, with an innocent expression on my face, I made my way into a park to find somewhere to rest and recuperate. I had brought some food with me for the journey, but it was nearly gone, and I needed to find my family urgently. I decided to risk asking for help and began studying the faces of people passing by to see if I could detect any friendliness in their faces. Most of the people had their heads down and scurried along self-absorbed; wrapped in their own private concerns. Eventually I spotted a middle-aged man whose head was up; his stroll was relaxed, and he smiled back when I made eye contact. I decided it was now or never and walked up to him. I spoke to him in

Russian, asking him if by any chance he knew of my family or where the area of the town was that I thought they lived in. He had never heard of them, but kindly gave me the name and address of a Jewish family who lived in the area I was looking for.

As soon as it was dark, I made my way to this Jewish house. After five days of travelling, mostly at night, I found myself fighting to keep awake. I made it to the doorway and sank down with exhaustion. The next thing I was aware of, it seemed to me that someone was rudely shaking me and hissing in my ear. It was one of those moments when you wake up somewhere unfamiliar and have that moment of panic as you wonder where on earth you are. The hissing in my ear was a woman who was trying to rouse me without making any noise. She helped me to my feet and pulled me into the house where I stood blinking in the light, trying to rally my thoughts.

"What are you doing sleeping in the doorway?" asked the woman with genuine concern. She had an oval face with an olive complexion and large kind brown eyes, she looked to be in her thirties; worry lines were already showing on her forehead.

"I have come from Poland," I began, "I am looking for my father's family. I know their name but not their exact address. We last had contact in 1922 so they may well have moved to a new address by now," I continued. The woman led me into a small room at the back of the house and told me to sit quietly whilst she fetched her husband.

"He may know your people," she said smiling as she closed the door. There was a collection of old family portraits on a wooden shelf, but the rest of the room was bare except for some simple furniture. I sat down and waited, hoping that I had not inadvertently walked into a trap. The woman came back a few minutes later with her husband in tow. He entered warily as if not sure what to expect and relaxed visibly when he saw that I really was just a boy.

"My wife tells me she recognises your Polish accent, so she believes your story," he said in a deep but soft voice, "Tell me who it is you are looking for and I will see what I can do to help." While I gave him all the details that I knew, his wife brought in a straw mattress that she lay on the floor of the room and some blankets.

"You can sleep here," she said, "and on no account must you go outside in daylight until we can find you some typically Russian clothes; if anyone recognises your foreign clothes you could be reported to the authorities," she warned.

"Every fifth person in Russia is an informer," chipped in the man, "In fact, even the schoolchildren watch their parents," he added darkly. "I have not heard of your father's cousin; it is possible some friends of ours who live in Lenin Street might know. I will take you there tomorrow night."

The following night when we arrived at the other family's house, they questioned me carefully to find out whether I was genuinely Polish and looking for my family. When they were quite sure of me, they made inquiries on my behalf and found that, although my family had previously lived in their area, they had since moved. Fortunately for me they found where Joseph and his wife were living and, once again under cover of darkness, I made my way to their house.

The door was opened by a young man in uniform who was clearly not my father's cousin but looked as if he might be some sort of guard. He looked very suspicious of me as I explained who I was and asked to see Joseph. Fortunately for me Joseph had not yet retired for the night and listened patiently while I told my story once again. After a few more questions, he clapped me on the shoulders, told me I was most welcome and hollered for his wife to come and see their relative. His wife, Aunt Stella was a most beautiful woman of about forty years of age. She wrapped me in a suffocating hug and wept tears of joy.

"You look just like your father," she said, smiling through the tears. "Looks more like his mother to me," said Joseph, "but I'm sure he'll look more manly when his face starts to sprout," he added playfully cuffing me on the chin. It soon became obvious to me that they had no children and no experience of how to treat them. But they were very kind and immediately arranged for some food and accommodation. The cook dished up a surprisingly good supper considering that there were supposed to be such shortages, and I tucked in with a healthy appetite. I slept like a log in the small bed chamber they set aside for my use and woke very late the next morning.

"Uncle Joseph has gone off to work, so I shall take care of you this morning," announced Aunt Stella unceremoniously walking into the room. "We shall have to get some clothes for you to wear, you can't go about with me dressed like that, and don't bother looking for anything to wear in these wardrobes, they're full of my furs," she added with evident satisfaction before leaving just as abruptly. Someone had put a bowl of warm soapy water and a towel on a table, so after a quick wash I dressed in the only clothes I had with me. Before I went to find my aunt, I had a quick peek in the wardrobes and sure enough, to my great surprise, they were stuffed with about ten mink coats.

Aunt Stella seemed to relish the excuse to go shopping, even if it wasn't for her own wardrobe. She chatted happily the whole time.

"Your uncle is an officer you know; he oversees the supply of all the building materials needed for the construction of large military installations. Of course, it's all hush hush so I don't even know what they're for. But don't worry we don't need him to drive us; we have a chauffeur," she said, clearly wanting to show off. I had not experienced that kind of behaviour in an adult before, but some instinct warned me not to tell her that before the invasion we had a chauffeur too. Compared to other households in the town, they lived in the luxury that I presumed was reserved for the Party elite. They had a lovely villa, just outside the town and seemed to have access to special shops designated for Party members where they could obtain anything they wished. Aunt Stella dressed me in more appropriate Russian-made clothing and made sure that the clothes I had arrived in were suitably disposed of.

Uncle Joseph was extremely clever; I knew that he had originally come from a wealthy land-owning family but had managed to conceal this so that he could make a career for himself in the Red Army. He and his wife Stella were also very popular, practically every night they entertained or went visiting, mostly with other army officers and their wives. During my stay I was always invited along. These parties consisted mainly of heavy drinking, unlimited food, music, and dancing. I was introduced to their friends as 'Vitaly from the West' using a familiar Russian name, and because they were with trusted friends no further questions were asked. At one of these riotous parties, I witnessed an intoxicated young officer playing Russian roulette with a loaded pistol; he survived. At another party, one of the officer's sons gave me a book about Lenin and the Spanish Civil War – this proved to be a life saver later in my trip.

"Here Vitaly, you can be in charge of the gramophone and records, they are after all from Poland," said Joseph, who in fact held his liquor remarkably well. "This is a special treasure, so it is a great honour for you to have the responsibility," he added with a wink. I had been amazed to see so many things that appeared to have been looted from Poland in their home. They had various small pieces of furniture, and Stella had rolls of dress material, mostly pure silk, and other expensive fabrics, probably manufactured in Lodz in Poland where they specialised in manufacturing all types of material. Joseph had at least fifteen superior quality Polish suits. They even had curtains and carpets that came from Poland. It seemed to me that the goods that had been stolen from our shops and homes had very quickly been distributed to the high-ranking officers and Party officials. When we were alone in the house, Joseph proudly showed me a bicycle and a Polish radio. "I have to keep that radio hidden in here," he said conspiratorially, "It is an offence for us to have a radio in case we listen to foreign propaganda. Most Russian families can only get cable radio with Russian programmes."

On Sunday, I asked about the possibility of going to church, but was told that the five Catholic churches and the Franciscan Monastery had all been closed after the Revolution and were mostly used as warehouses. The Orthodox church had been demolished and the building material used to build a school. Instead, Joseph and Stella took me to meet another family in the town. These people kissed and hugged me, and even cried, because they had not met anyone from Poland for so many years. Although this family had continued secretly to speak Polish at home, they were not allowed to speak their own language in public. The punishment, I was told, would be deportation to Siberia. The town authorities denied that there were any Polish people living there.

I stayed with Uncle Joseph and Aunt Stella for about three weeks. Having been fitted out with Russian-made clothing, I was able to walk around unnoticed in the daytime. I took the opportunity to have a good look around in case I might find out something useful to pass on when I got back home. I explored the army barracks that were mostly cavalry. I also got as near to the military aerodrome as I dared and tried to count the number of planes they had. No one took much notice of me because I was just a boy. I discovered that the planes were mostly bombers and in fact were some of those which had bombed Poland at the beginning of the invasion.

In the old Polish cemetery, dating back to the sixteenth century, I found graves of generals, colonels, and members of the aristocracy from the days of Imperial Russia. There was a woman in the cemetery who noticed me looking at the graves.

"Are you interested in the Polish graves?" she asked, evidently curious about my interest but nevertheless wary of my motive.

"Yes, I have some Polish ancestry," I said, hoping that my Polish accent would not give me away too easily. As she gave a broad smile, her whole face seemed to light up.

"Ah, I also have Polish ancestry," she admitted, "I am a schoolteacher. If you are interested in history, I have a wonderful collection of books and magazines printed before the war. Would you like to see them?" I couldn't think what harm I might come to with this charming lady, so I nodded and followed her to her small and simple but elegantly furnished home. Her books and magazines were a real surprise, I hadn't realised that so many Polish families had lived there in the past.

"Under the Imperial Russian authorities, we were permitted to live our own political and social life. Before the war the Catholic churches here organised us and kept our cultural life active as well as our faith," she said with evident nostalgia. "We were allowed to practice our own religion, print our own periodicals and in every way lead a free life," she added. "I expect you already know that most of the land in this region used to be owned by Polish noblemen, then after the Bolshevik Revolution the land was confiscated, and the owners sent to Siberia." I nodded, but in my head recalled Father's account of what had happened to my own grandparents. The schoolteacher must have been glad to have someone to talk to; she continued to give me a history lesson of the area. She told me that after the Revolution, the Bolsheviks wanted to intimidate the Polish families left in the area, so they dug up the bodies of Polish priests from their graves and put them on display to prove that religion was finished and could not help the people in future. I can't imagine she would have made up such a gruesome story.

Where the river Horyn flowed through the town, it had been dammed up to provide electricity for the town. The large military installation that Uncle Joseph was overseeing the construction of was nearby. He was very proud that Stalin had personally authorised the work and showed me the letters and documents signed by Stalin. These documents meant that Joseph had priority to obtain any materials that he required. An underground storage area had already been filled with large amounts of ammunition and other articles ready for later, when, according to the officers, Stalin planned to invade Germany once he had Poland safely settled under his control. I decided it was time to return home.

I was able to walk in the daytime on my return journey as my replacement clothing made me inconspicuous. This meant that I had the opportunity to see for myself the enormous collective farms that had replaced the pre-revolution small holdings. The fields that had grown wheat in the summer had now been ploughed and I counted over a hundred tractors on one enormous piece of land alone. I was shocked to see all that machinery, used for threshing corn, had been left outside to rust. I guessed that no one bothered about state-owned property, and I saw many other examples of machinery and tools outside decaying through neglect.

The houses where the collective farmers lived were also neglected and looked as if they had never been painted. The farm workers were in rags; there seemed to be shortages of every kind. As I passed one hardware shop, I glanced in the window and at least half of the shelves were stacked up with boxes of matches and nothing else. But there were photographs of Lenin and Stalin, and propaganda magazines for sale. Their pictures were displayed everywhere, hanging amongst red flags. I kept wondering why Russia wanted to have Poland when they already had so much land of their own that was totally neglected.

Having walked for days undetected, I was taken by surprise when a civilian spotted me as I was approaching the border crossing. He called the attention of the two border guards to me, and without any discussion, they arrested me. Still not speaking a word, they stuck their bayonets up against my ribs and marched me into the guardroom. They then proceeded to interrogate me for several hours.

"Why are you crossing the border? What information do you have? Who is your informant? Which organisation do you work for? Where are you headed? Where have you been?" The same questions were repeated, over and over, without them showing any intention of listening to my answers.

"If you do not tell us the truth, you will be shot as a spy," said one of them angrily.

"The crossing rules state that the punishment for the crime of illegally crossing the border is ten years' imprisonment," said the other, presumably hoping to get me to confess to the lesser crime.

"I visited Russia because I have always been interested in Russia, having learned the language at school. So, as soon as I had the chance, I decided to see it for myself," I told them. "I have an uncle in Zaslaw that I wanted to visit. Look, I can prove my love for Russia, I have a book all about Comrade Lenin." I took the book out of the bag I had been carrying with the supplies Aunt Stella had given me for my journey and handed it to them. They examined the book thoroughly from cover to cover, obviously looking for secret writing between the lines. They found nothing and angrily threatened me again with a revolver. One of them wrote a statement.

"Here, you must sign this statement," I was told.

"What's the matter with you? I've just been visiting my uncle," I replied, refusing to sign the statement, although I was terrified, and trying to pretend it was all a joke.

"You will stay locked in here overnight and we'll see if you feel any different in the morning. The dog can keep you company," growled one of the men as he let an Alsatian into the cell with me. Every time I moved, even a finger, the dog growled at me. The guards had deliberately left a window wide open, but I knew that I would be shot if I tried to jump through and get away. I believed that was what they were hoping I would do. In the morning, they opened the door.

"You are free," they said. They took me to the border and practically threw me across. That was my first visit to Stalinist Russia.

CHAPTER 13

DEPORTATION (FEBRUARY 1940)

Sometime in the middle of November, Father returned home. Mother woke me in the middle of the night, whispering in my ear and telling me to keep quiet.

"Just listen carefully, your father has been badly wounded in the leg but has somehow managed to get home. Come with me to our bedroom without making any noise; be careful where you tread, we can't risk using a light in case any of the neighbours sees and informs," she said in an urgent undertone. With arms outstretched in front while my eyes adjusted to the darkness, I followed Mother into their bedroom. I could just make out where Father lay stretched out on the bed, still fully clothed, with one arm thrown over his face, covering his eyes. His wounded leg had been covered by a blanket. I guess Mother had already cleaned and dressed it before she came to get me. It would be essential to prevent any infection as it was too dangerous to call out a doctor. Father lowered his arm and looked in our direction as we entered the room on tiptoe. Even in the darkness I could see that he had changed; I was shocked at his appearance. He was unshaven and unwashed, and his face looked thin and gaunt from the pain. He was evidently totally exhausted, and although relieved to be home, was depressed and fidgety.

"Where have you been?" I asked, "Are you allowed to say?"

"I won't be giving any secrets away to tell you that when our army stopped fighting, I escaped into the forest with several other men. We spent some time recovering abandoned munitions for future use. It just wasn't possible to fight on two fronts," he groaned, "It would have been a senseless waste of manpower to continue fighting; we had no choice but to capitulate." Mother laid a hand gently on his shoulder and beckoned me over, saying,

"Say goodnight now, Viktor. You can have a proper catch up tomorrow when your father has had a chance to rest."

In the morning, we found out that Father had been helping to establish the underground resistance force that we Boy Scouts had been collecting information for. He was just as interested to hear what we had been up to as I was about him.

Soon after this we learned from friends that the occupying Bolshevik officials had a list of local people who were to be arrested. They were making house-to-house searches day and night looking for particular people on their lists and anyone who they thought would oppose the new system, especially anyone connected in any way with the underground resistance army. Our home was searched at least once a week, during the night. The door was forced open and Russian soldiers would trample through the house terrifying Anna, nanny, and the cook, as they opened drawers and cupboards and turned out the contents while we were held at gunpoint. Each time they would take something away with them. We presumed that Father would be on their list because of his previous connections with the Imperial Russian family. Although he had so far evaded detection, Father decided to go back into the forest with several other officers where they were organising groups of resistance. It was my job to take food out to them and act as messenger.

"Remember to go a different way from yesterday," said Mother on one of my early excursions, "If you go on your bicycle somewhere fast, you could leave it hidden and go the rest of the way on foot after you have lost anyone that might be following," she suggested. "And if you think you have been followed, whatever you do don't risk giving away Father's location, even if you have to abandon your trip." Mother hadn't known all the things we Boy Scouts had already been getting up to and how you develop a sort of instinct about being followed; you can feel a person's eyes on you, especially when you're their prey. On many occasions I was followed by informers, most probably from the minority group of Ukrainian nationalists who were by then cooperating with the Russians, but I always managed to change my route and times of visits.

In the new year, the weather deteriorated. Although we had tropical summers in our region, the winters were arctic. The men in the forest dug themselves a deep bunker, but it was extremely cold and damp. When the temperature dropped to minus twenty-five centigrade, Father had to return home. It had become impossible to sleep outside in those conditions, and Mother and I persuaded Father to return home, if only for a short time, to recuperate and rest.

In the middle of the night, in the early hours of Saturday February 10th, a date that many thousands of Poles will have etched into their memory, a large posse of Russian troops encircled our house. We were woken by the tremendous noise being made as they broke down the front door with their rifle butts and hammers. Father had immediately fled up to the attic where he kept hidden a hand grenade and a revolver. Mother, Anna, and I were forced at gunpoint into the kitchen and made to stand shivering with fright and cold with our hands over our heads, dressed only in our nightclothes.

An NKVD officer began pulling mattresses off the beds and upturning drawers and wardrobes. The rest of the soldiers scattered through the house searching everywhere for evidence of weapons, and we presumed, for Father. We could hear the heavy footsteps going up towards the attic and then heard with horror the voice of one man shouting "Weapons!" I braced myself for the sound of shots or an explosion, but Father had not tried to defend himself with his weapons, and moments later he was dragged down the stairs with guns pushed up against him. He was made to lie on the floor face down and his hands were tied behind his back. Anna started crying uncontrollably.

"Why didn't he use the grenade or his revolver?" I asked Mother in a confused whisper.

"He probably thought it would cause more trouble for us," she whispered back, "don't ask him; it was a difficult decision."

When they had completed their search for weapons, the NKVD officer opened a briefcase that he had brought with him into the house and took out a large book. He read out our names and the warrant for our arrest, saying,

"You are not local people, you are enemies of the state, therefore, by order of the Soviet Union, you will be relocated to another town," and paused for a moment to allow his words to sink in, then added, "You will leave immediately." He then left us to the supervision of the soldiers who told us we had twenty minutes to get dressed and pack some clothes and food enough for one day. One young soldier whispered to Mother,

"Take as much as possible, there is nothing where you are going."

He spoke in Russian, but we all understood. Mother stuffed what food she could get hold of in the short time in a bag and we all dressed as warmly as we could; the temperature outside was at least minus twenty-five centigrade. As we were herded into the street, our lovely big dog began to howl terribly because we were leaving him. One of the soldiers shot him dead. We were put into a lorry and driven to a local railway station. From there our destination could only be East. It was the harshest winter for many years; many people arrived at the station on sledges. A heavy snow was falling, driven by a strong wind, so that the people were already frozen to the bone before they even arrived at the station. No one had eaten breakfast; nursing babies and infants had not been fed and the sick had been dragged from their beds. If this had all happened in summer more people may have survived, but it was the coldest night of the year.

There was a long train of numbered cattle trucks. A few were already loaded with people. I could see faces peering through tiny openings. The NKVD officer at the station called us bloodsuckers, and said with a kind of grim satisfaction, "You are making the poor people in our country suffer, so we have to eliminate you." Then he read out the names on his list and we were led to our assigned truck where armed soldiers guarded the doors. This took just a few minutes and then the wagons were locked or screwed shut from the outside.

There were many other people from our town and the surrounding area, including families with children; the children were crying. Eventually there were so many of us in that truck that we could only stand up. There was one small, grated frost-covered window. There was a hole in the floor for a toilet.

The train stayed in the station for two weeks, without any sanitation other than the awful hole and no water. The cold was extreme; the walls were covered in frost. The only way to sleep was to take it in turns to lie on the floor in between legs of the people standing. Older people simply couldn't stand up for long and collapsed onto the floor in heaps. Children sat on laps to take up less space and others crouched with their legs curled up. There was at least one benefit of the cold, the stench from the hole in the corner would have been intolerable in warmer months. At first people tried to use the hole only at night because of the lack of privacy, but eventually we were able to rig up a blanket to permit some modesty. We were not fed for those two weeks, but some of us had brought food and that was shared around. One person had a loaf, others a brick of butter or a hunk of meat or salted pork. When we begged for water, the inhuman reply had its intended effect on us,

"You bloodsuckers don't need any water; you will die in any case."

If anyone tried to escape, they were bayoneted to the ground, the men in charge observing that a bullet was too expensive to waste on us.

At the end of the two weeks, when the whole train was packed with residents from Rovno and families from the surrounding settlements, we started our journey towards Moscow. As we crossed the border, people shed tears as we left our beautiful homeland behind us. When we made a stop, one of the other boys, who was trying to keep a track of our route called out to a guard.

"Where is the next station?"

We all heard the reply,

"For you this is the end of the world." It certainly felt that it was the end of our world.

"Why are they doing this?" Anna asked over and over, repeating the same question that everyone else was asking themselves.

54

"Because they think we will oppose their way of life; because they have a different system," answered Father, trying to sound as if their behaviour towards us was just a misunderstanding rather than what was more likely a hatred born of envy.

Just outside Moscow, the train halted again, and we stayed there for six days, not knowing where we were being taken to. I called out in Russian to one of the guards,

"Where are we being taken to?"

"The land of the white bear," we were told.

Occasionally, we were given salted fish but no fresh water. Wherever there was a small gap between the slats of the wagon, we put our hands out and caught snow that we could drink as it melted. The fish was very stale.

"I can't eat it," wailed Anna, "It must be about twenty years old."

"You must try," Mother encouraged, "I agree it tastes utterly repulsive, but you must eat," she insisted.

"Try holding your nose while you eat," I suggested, "It's a bit easier if you don't have to smell it at the same time." The fish was so unpalatable that many people were immediately sick on tasting it. There was no milk available for the very young children who could not eat the fish, so some of them died on that journey. Some of the elderly, or sick also died while the train was still standing outside Moscow.

The only way to keep up our spirits was to say prayers for our salvation and then entertain ourselves by singing and telling stories – anything to occupy our minds. One person tried to cheer us up with jokes, but they fell on deaf ears. We persuaded Father to tell us some of the stories he used to tell us. When he ran out of ideas, Mother suggested that we tell the story of Peter and the Wolf together, giving each one of us a role; Peter, the wolf, the cat, the duck and so on. Father had brought a gramophone record of the story and music back from Warsaw about a year before, and we had listened to it many times. Mother, being a musician, could remember all the themes. She began the narration but was interrupted by a well-spoken but angry gentleman.

"What are you doing? Don't you know that the composer, that Prokofiev, is a dirty Russian?" he objected.

"Music is a universal language," said Mother calmly, "It transcends politics, or race, or religion, or nationality. Not all Russians hate us, and we should not hate all Russians." Our little rendition of the story occupied us for a short while, but it was hard to maintain the enthusiasm, most people slipped into a kind of detached withdrawn state of existence.

One or two of the occupants completely lost it. One woman, probably in her thirties, began to wet herself, talking aloud to herself, muttering the same phrases over and over.

"Why is this happening to me? What could I have done to stop this? I know I must be guilty of something; I will confess to anything." She even began to tell us that she was someone else entirely, living in some sort of parallel world.

"What's happening to her?" I asked Father.

"It's something I have seen before, when troops go into battle, they can lose their reason because of the acute anxiety," he told me. Others were affected too, some of the older men had angry outbursts, complaining of abdominal or chest pains, nausea, and headaches. It was easy to empathise with those who became paranoid, detached from reality, or began to hallucinate.

After we left Moscow, the train headed east for Siberia. We were given soup in buckets once a day and a small hunk of black bread to keep us alive. From time to time the guards opened the truck, counted us, and took away the dead. Imagine the sorrow of the families when a member of their family was taken away, not knowing whether they would be buried or just thrown to the wolves. So many people died on that journey. When the grandmother of one poor family perished from the conditions, we had only just left a station, so it was likely to be a long while before we stopped again. People began complaining.

"The old lady is taking up too much space," muttered one woman struggling to keep her children from using the old woman's body as a seat. The old lady's son, visibly weeping, pleaded for his mother to be left alone, but the complaints continued.

"It's unhygienic; she will cause disease," someone else said. The poor man had to watch as the grate was removed from the small window and his mother's body was unceremoniously pushed out of the window. I can only imagine how he and his family suffered.

We travelled for two months to Siberia. Eventually we came to the end of our journey at Krasnoyarsk. The railway guards had not yet had orders regarding what to do with us. Many of us were in a very bad state of health and the guards gave us a little more food. I was so hungry that I felt as though I could have eaten a whole horse. I was also desperately worried about Mother; I felt as though I should have been able to help her more, but there was nothing I could do; for some strange reason I was filled with guilt, convinced that somehow all these terrible events were all my fault. All of us had become increasingly withdrawn. I remember my voice croaking when I did speak, I thought it was because I was forgetting how to have a conversation, but it was probably malnutrition.

When the orders came through from the authorities, a lot of people came from collective farms with sledges and horses. We travelled nearly a week until we reached our destination in the endless Siberian taiga forests near the shores of the Yenisei River. On our arrival we were settled into old barracks, I remember the sound of the children screaming and the ladies crying. The camp was already full of Russian prisoners. They were overjoyed to see us, and immediately started to teach us all the tricks of survival. Once inside our accommodation, Mother said,

"Right, this is your home now, make yourself comfortable."

CHAPTER 14

SIBERIA (1940)

Over the duration of the journey, I had found myself constantly thinking about food, talking about food, and dreaming about food. The one slice of black clay-like bread and infrequent bowls of thin lukewarm vegetable soup had barely kept us alive, and this meagre diet continued. The food was horrible. We were given about two square inches of bread each per day. The bread wasn't made of wheat, but with various kinds of poor-quality cereals. Nearly every day we had a bowl of fish soup, made from salted fish, and like the fish we had been given on the journey, it was very malodourous.

The first time I tried to eat this fish soup, the smell caused me to retch uncontrollably.

"I can't eat this," I said with utter revulsion.

One of the Russian prisoners, a large gruff man that reminded me of the big brown bears roaming the forests, tried to encourage me to eat.

"You will soon get used to it," he said through his thick beard, "and begin to like it; you need it to stop the night blindness" he added nodding, reminding me even more of a bear. Not yet sure what night blindness meant, I followed his advice to try to eat it however horrible. I managed to make myself a peg by splitting a short green stick and put it on my nose so that I could eat the soup without having to smell it. Once the weather warmed up, those of us who worked outside were able to pick a few blue berries or black berries, and sometimes even mushrooms to supplement our awful diet.

Our camp was near to the river Yenisei in the Putorana Mountains, but some of our people were sent further east, even as far as the river Lena in eastern Siberia. Everyone in the camp, from the age of fourteen to sixty-five had to work. The Soviet motto was: 'He who does not work does not eat.' Some of our original group were sent to work in the mines, but during the day, most of us worked in the forest, felling trees, and clearing the shrubs and bushes. Trees that had been felled were then cut into boards with blunt saws. Some of the women were made to drive carts pulled by oxen to transport the logs. We were expected to work for twelve hours each day. I worked with another boy, Tomasz; we had only one axe between us. We were told to cut down ten trees or we would have nothing to eat. I remember them waving a potato at us and saying,

"You haven't cut enough; no food for your today." So we had to work terribly hard to earn our food. We were made to build new barracks for the next batch of prisoners expected to arrive. I wondered why so many Polish prisoners were being brought here and who would work the land back home. One day I put my question to one of the more senior guards.

"The Soviet Union has decided to move all of the Polish speaking people from that part of the Soviet Republics to work for us here and open up the Siberian waste lands for the glory of the Union."

None of us were criminals, although we were accused of being 'enemies of the State', and neither could many of us be described as prisoners of war; very few were soldiers, and none, other than Father who kept it secret, were officers. We were, I told Tomasz, "Slave labourers like the people of Israel had been in Egypt at the time of Moses."

There was a wire fence around the camp, and although it wasn't guarded as such, no one was allowed beyond it aside from the forest workers. Our guards were from the Kalmyck and Mongolian regions, both oriental tribes and, according to the locals, feared for their reputation of cruelty and indifference to human suffering. When we had first arrived, one of these guards had warned us.

"Do not try to escape; even the wolves are starving in these forests; you would not get very far."

On one occasion, Tomasz was trying to get a recalcitrant horse to pull its load. He got himself a flexible stick to use like a whip in the way he had probably done before on his farm at home. The supervisor noticed and shouted at him,

"Don't do that! The horses are precious; people aren't."

Children under the age of fourteen went to school in the camp. They were supposed to learn the Russian language and received political indoctrination and propaganda to get them to believe in communism and reject capitalism. At least they were given some soup at school. My sister Anna was a very clever girl; she seemed to have a photographic memory of which I was very jealous. The authorities decided to take the clever children away to Moscow. Poor Mother, she didn't want her to go and wept angry tears of frustration.

"At least she will be properly fed in Moscow; she won't have to work in the forests like Viktor and the rest of us and with a good education she may have a chance of a good future," Father had said trying to console Mother. But we missed Anna terribly, especially Mother.

As more prisoners were brought in, our group was moved on to clear further areas of virgin forest. We were moving steadily in an eastwardly direction the whole time. After many months of travelling, and clearing forests and undergrowth, we were finally moved to an area so remote that there were not even any deserted barracks or huts for our sleeping accommodation. We had to clear the area, fell trees, and hurriedly build our own huts as a priority.

The seasons changed very quickly in Siberia. One day there was hard frost and the next day Spring arrived. The sun shone, the ground started to thaw, and within a couple of days Spring flowers appeared. The blue snowdrops, lilac lungwort, pink and purple primroses, and bright yellow coltsfoot were a shock to the senses after the seemingly endless grey and white of the winter. But with the warmer weather came a new cause for misery – bed bugs. The bugs made their nests in the moss that covered the ceiling inside the barracks. During the night they would fall on us while we lay in our bunks. I also learned about the existence of the evil insect called a louse when I noticed something whitish crawling down inside someone's collar. We were soon infested with lice and bed bugs, and nothing was done to get rid of them. They spread disease and of course there was no medical care in the camp. The old, the sick, and the young died.

Winter also came very quickly. I found some frost-shrunken rosehips that looked rather like prunes and shared these with Tomasz, but within a few days nothing could be found in the snow that fell continuously day and night. The weather was intensely cold, and our clothes and shoes had begun to wear out. When we complained to our guards about the cold and lack of clothing, we were given some old sacks to wrap our feet in and somehow make ourselves clothing.

The Russian prisoners showed us how to protect our feet using the sacking. The one I thought of as Brown Bear showed me what to do.

"First you wrap your feet with one layer of the sacking," he said, demonstrating on his own feet. "Now we get another layer of sacking and between the two layers, we stuff straw or moss." He pulled some of the moss from the walls and padded between the two layers of sacking. "Next we put it in water."

"But won't it just disintegrate?" I asked doubtfully.

"You have to put it outside to freeze," he explained patiently, "and then it will hold together, for a while at least."

The trouble was the sacking was thin and we had to keep remaking the outer covering of these boots. What made it worse was that they were very clumsy to walk in; we could only walk very slowly in them. Sometime later, we were given some old lorry tyres and we were able to make ourselves shoes from these.

"We're very lucky to have some clever shoemakers here," Father had said proudly, showing me how one of our men had managed to shave off a slice of the tyre and attach the rubber to the soles of his sacking shoes. This new device made our shoes much stronger and kept our feet dry.

We were still cutting trees, clearing undergrowth, and now also breaking stones ready for roadmaking. During the winter in camp, the cold was frightening. We reckoned the temperature could drop to minus seventy-five centigrade. The incredibly low temperatures seemed to slow the heart and it made you feel unbearably sleepy. Even during the daytime, while I was working, I felt as if I was only half awake.

"Listen carefully, Viktor," Father told me when the temperature first began to plumet, "The greatest danger to your life is if you sit down to rest and fall asleep. You could be dead within just ten minutes from hypothermia." From then on, I made sure I was always working close by to someone else, usually Tomasz, so that we could agree to keep each other awake. The more experienced Russian prisoners, who had already survived several winters, advised us to organise ourselves so that one person in each hut kept awake all through the night to build up the fire.

"If the fire goes out, not one person in the hut will survive the night," they warned. It was the men that got this job, and they took it in turns, organising a rota. Even with all these precautions, there were many deaths. Death seemed to be all around us; we youngsters grew up very quickly in these surroundings. Every morning our first job was to take out the bodies of the people who had died from weakness, dysentery, or general malnutrition. Some nights as many as forty people could die, mostly the very old or the very young.

It was our responsibility to bury those who had died, and this was also shared out fairly. In the winter the land was so frozen that we had to light a fire on the chosen resting place to soften the ground. This could take hours, so we boys were often left in charge of keeping the fires going while the men continued with their usual work. Tomasz and I had a chance for conversation during these times, and it helped to keep us awake. I told Tomasz about my home life, and he told me about his life on the settler farm that turned out to have been just on the other side of the river Horyn.

"We might even have seen each other before, fishing or boating on the river," he had said nostalgically. Sometimes it was the women who took over this job. But even after lighting fires, the ground couldn't just be dug up like normal earth, it had to be chopped up. Even in the summer only the top six inches seemed to thaw. As a result, the graves were of necessity very shallow.

The constant proximity to death meant that we had to rely on our Christian faith, the only source of hope in this hell on earth. We weren't allowed to set up any kind of permanent place of worship or anything resembling an altar. The Bolsheviks had outlawed all religion, but they couldn't prevent us praying. Every night, before we settled down for sleep, we held organised prayers. Some people recited passages from the Gospels or the Psalms that they had learned by heart. When the prayers started, so did the sobbing; people poured out their hearts to God. We prayed that Almighty God would deliver us from this hell in which we found ourselves. Those of us that could remember the words softly sang hymns. This was a tremendous comfort to our people. The Bolsheviks had a six-day working week, but the rest day did not always fall on a Sunday, but our family continued to mark Sunday and found time to pray together as we had done at home. Our faith gave us strength and hope, and when I think back, I wonder how people survived without any faith to support them.

The Soviets did not celebrate Christmas; being a religious festival it had been abolished in keeping with the Marxist ideology that says, 'Religion is the opium of the people.' Consequently, Christmas was a workday. The Bolsheviks had a holiday on January 1st so that they could still give gifts to their children. Even before the Revolution, the Russians celebrated Christmas on a different day, the Orthodox Church held Christmas two weeks later than ours. The guards didn't prevent us singing our beautiful Polish carols, but when Christmas arrived it was difficult not to feel sorry for ourselves.

"What on earth can we use to provide some sort of food for our Christmas Eve celebrations?" Mother had asked. It was a rhetorical question; she didn't expect an answer. For us, Christmas Eve is the main celebration of the Christmas period, and it begins when the first star is sighted. At home, in Poland, we would have celebrated with a real feast. We always had a meal consisting of twelve kinds of food, one for each of the Apostles. Our parties would finish in time for us all to attend Midnight Mass at our local church. The children in the camp school were allowed to have pens and paper, so they were able to draw Christmas cards for their parents and it looked as if that was going to be the only sign of Christmas.

I worked all day alongside Tomasz and the rest of the forest workers as usual on December 24th. When we returned to barracks for the evening meal, anticipating a hunk of bread and fish soup, we were told that we were very lucky as there would be a small piece of meat for everyone to go with the usual soup. I was very surprised, even shocked. When we went for our meal, everyone received a tiny piece of well-roasted (almost burnt) very lean meat.

"How is it that we have meat?" I asked Mother.

"Some of the men cooked it for us; they roasted it secretly – as a surprise," she answered, evidently uplifted by this small Christmas gesture. Looking around I noticed that some people seemed to have a piece of leg from an animal that I didn't recognise.

"But what sort of animal is it that we're eating?" I persisted, feeling puzzled. One of the men overheard my questions and shouted across.

"It's probably a bear, although it must have been a baby judging by the size of my piece," he said laughing and licking his precious piece of meat to make it last longer. It was, I had to admit, possible to catch and kill a bear if you were really lucky, but it would take several strong men and a great deal of courage to do so. I knew that it wasn't bear; there had been no opportunity to catch one, the legs were too small, and if it truly had been bear that we were eating so enthusiastically, we would have had a larger portion each. Regardless of where it came from, we all ate our bit of meat and thoroughly enjoyed it.

A few days later, I became aware that one of the guards was looking for his dog. The animal was clearly his responsibility, but he was also evidently fond of him, hunting everywhere and even asking us prisoners if we had seen him.

"He must have wandered off when I took him off his leash for some exercise," he said, "I can't understand it; he is such an obedient dog."

"If he jumped the wire and went into the forest, the wolves may have got him," suggested one of the other guards, "even an Alsatian wouldn't stand a chance against a pack."

With horror and revulsion, I realised that some of our men must have killed and cooked this guard's Alsatian dog; the one who kept guard on our own barracks. It must have been this dog that we had eaten with such relish. I found it hard to believe that our people could be so cruel to such a beautiful animal; I guess it had reminded me of our own beautiful guard dog that I had loved and missed so much.

"I know we are pretty much starving," I later complained to Father, "but my stomach turns over and I feel sick every time I think about the poor animal."

"The instinct to survive is very strong," he said without trying to justify what had happened, he was simply making an observation about life, "and in some it is stronger than others. I pray that it will be strong in you and that you survive no matter what ordeal you might have to face." There was a deep sorrow in his eyes as he spoke, and it flashed through my mind that he had already undergone ordeals that I could not yet imagine. We sat together in silence, absorbed in our own thoughts, but sharing that warmth of understanding, a rare moment of oneness, that can happen between kindred spirits.

Mulling it over in the coming days, I felt very sad that we seemed to have sunk so low as to kill and eat a dog. I told the women who were responsible for cooking,

"In future, if you give me anything to eat, it must not be dog."

The guards must have become suspicious, because after the disappearance of our guard dog, they never again allowed any of the dogs to be let out for exercise unless accompanied by a guard. After all, they were very well trained and valuable animals.

A few days after Christmas, I was given the job of cleaning the guard's sleeping accommodation. This was considered quite a privilege and often an opportunity.

"Keep your eyes open for anything that you can safely bring back; scraps of food or material for mending clothes and such like," Mother told me with some excitement and even anticipation. Being young, I was often able to get into places that were normally forbidden to adults. If anything could stick to my fingers or fit in my pocket, it belonged to me!

Whilst cleaning their kitchen, I found a whole lot of fish heads to be thrown on the rubbish tip. This was out of bounds for the prisoners. I filled my pockets with these fish heads and even stuffed them inside my shirt so that I could carry as many as possible back to Mother. On the way back to the barracks, the smell of the fish made me feel so hungry that I started to eat one of them in its raw state; I got through quite a large head before I got to the barracks. A short while later I was retching and being sick. Mother shook her head in disbelief,

"Did you eat one of those raw fish heads?" she asked unsympathetically. "You would not be able to digest the hard flesh," she told me.

"But I was so hungry; perhaps that one had gone off," I moaned.

"There is a very good reason why we humans cook fish," she said, "I shall cook the others and you'll see that they are perfectly good."

The next day I was so ill that I could not work and did not dare move in case it brought on a further bout of retching.

"You had better lie by the fire to keep warm," recommended Mother when she noticed me shivering as my temperature began dropping from inactivity. Meanwhile, she cooked all the remaining fish heads, and with small bits of bread saved by some of the others, made an almost-delicious fish soup.

One memorable evening, when we were about to have our evening meal, we heard a terrible row coming from one of the other barracks. When anything out of the ordinary occurred, something to alleviate the monotony of everyday life, it generated great excitement, and so those that could rushed outside to see what was happening. We could clearly hear the upraised angry voices of two men. Apparently, the person who was responsible for sharing out the bread in their barracks had evidently cut the pieces slightly unequally.

"I tell you it isn't fair," yelled one angry voice, adding a volley of expletives. Most of the women disinterestedly went back inside at this point. We had heard it all before; these kinds of arguments about fair portions were a regular occurrence. But the volume of shouting increased, and we could hear sounds as if furniture was being thrown around and several people exited the barracks in a hurry, clearly frightened by the escalating violence. A kind of hush fell on those of us who were still outside listening; I expected to see the guards coming to investigate the commotion at any moment, but no one came. Eventually one of the men came out and ran off in the direction of the shed that housed the tools for the forestry work. Moments later he returned carrying one of the chopping tools. At this point Father marched me firmly back inside, realising that the situation had become extremely dangerous. We later found out that the man with the chopper had struck his opponent on the head and killed him.

When the others returned, they were subdued. One man, shaking his head muttering,

"They shouldn't laugh. Did you hear what they said? 'Well, that's one less capitalist'."

"Prisoners here have killed for a slice of bread before," said one of the long-time Russian inhabitants, "The authorities never interfere, they just tell you to improve yourselves," he added, mimicking the camp Commissar, "You must improve yourselves, and become decent citizens and then you will be set free!"

Another time there was a commotion in the guard's barracks. Again, people surged into the vicinity demonstrating the morbid curiosity of the mob. From inside our own barracks, we could hear repeated gun shots, and fearful of the cause, and possible reprisals, we stayed inside.

"If it is something we need to know about, we'll find out soon enough," Father had said grimly. We did find out; it was one of the friendlier Russians who told us what had happened.

"Some of our Russian prisoners attacked the guards hoping to steal some food. They had made some weapons for themselves and killed several of the guards. The shots we heard were the reprisals; the authorities executed about thirty Russian prisoners," he said with a resigned shrug of the shoulders.

Then we had to bury them. It was hard to believe how badly the Russian authorities treated their own people. As foreigners, and as they said of us 'enemies of the state', we would expect harsh treatment, but we never expected to see their own people being treated like animals.

The political Commissar would make unexpected visits to inspect the guards to make sure they were maintaining control over us prisoners. On one occasion, he arrived to find the guards all drunk. He was justifiably angry, but we were shocked by his reaction. Inevitably there was something of an uproar so the whole incident was witnessed by many of us who piled out to see what was going on. The Commissar furiously ordered replacement guards to be sent for. Then he hauled out the guard's commanding officer, accused him of dereliction of duty, and shot him on the spot. We were appalled to see the terrible things happening even to the Russian people. The Commissar turned his enraged gaze towards us,

"This is justice in Soviet Russia," he spat with utter loathing on his face.

One day, what seemed like a breath of fresh air and sunshine came to visit. My sister Anna was allowed to visit us in the prison camp. In Moscow, we were told, there were terrible shortages and she had caught tuberculosis for which there were no available medicines at that time. Ironically, she told us that at the school in Moscow they were teaching her what she needed to know so that she could one day become a doctor. Mother fussed over her for the precious three days she was allowed to stay. It was heart-breaking listening to Anna's persistent coughing, often bringing up blood-stained phlegm, and seeing her thin emaciated face with dark circles around her eyes. Of course, Mother was overjoyed to see her but asked,

"Why have they brought her here? This is no place for her to get well; I can't understand it."

Father was depressed and Mother wept inconsolably for days when Anna left again, both were convinced that they would never see their precious daughter alive again. Somehow the darkness of our prison seemed more intense after she had gone, and we all felt a sense of deep foreboding about the future.

At some point in our imprisonment, each person was called into the political Commissar's office, interrogated, and given a form to sign. On this form, the reason for our 'resettlement' was to be filled in by each prisoner. No one knew what the real reason was, but the authorities would only accept one answer: 'enemies of the state', and the sentence for this was either ten or twenty-five-years imprisonment. The guards were inhumanly brutal, and after our people returned from their interrogation, they were hardly recognisable from cuts and bruises, their faces swollen out of all proportion and sometimes even with teeth missing.

All of us over the age of fourteen were interrogated in turn, and as time wore on the inevitable day loomed ever closer. We would simply be told to sign the statement admitting our faults and accepting our sentence.

I still relive the nightmare from witnessing one of the prisoners, a man in his forties, when he returned from his interrogation. This poor man was dragged back to barracks and dumped on the floor. As he rolled over, we could see with horror that his eyes were falling out of their sockets and his whole body was red with blood. I can still hear his pitiful moans as several women tried to find a way to help him.

"We can't move him," said one of the women, cautioning the others, "I think his arm is broken, and probably his ribs too." Letting him lie still, they tried their best to wrap him in sacking padded with moss.

"Wouldn't sign," he managed to say, "Jumped on me with their heavy boots and gouged out my eyes," he sobbed with the pain. "Have pity; I can't stand the pain; just kill me," he pleaded. It was unbearable to listen to. There was very little our people could do to help him, only press cold snow on his bruises to help deaden the pain. He died after two days, and we had to bury him. This had been a warning to the rest of us of what would happen if we refused to sign our statements.

These interrogations, by the political Commissar, went on daily until everyone in the camp had been questioned. Mock evidence was prepared, and a sentence prescribed. It was only a matter of time before it was my turn, and the treatment I experienced was the standard treatment for all of us, men and women alike. At about two o'clock in the morning I found myself being dragged forcibly from my bunk and knew that this was it. I was marched at gun point into the Commissar's office where he stood on the far side of a large table.

"Strip," ordered one of the guards, and I began slowly to take off my outer garments and then hesitated.

"Everything," ordered the guard. Shivering uncontrollably now, with cold and fear, I removed the last few items of my protection and stood exposed before them. On the table were set out what looked like a variety of instruments of torture; just the sight of them was terrifying. Two of the guards grabbed hold of me and forced me backwards on to the table and strapped me down. Then the questioning began. The Commissar held up what he said was my report.

"You fought against the glorious Soviet Republics between 1917 to 1919," he stated.

"I wasn't born until 1925," I said politely, thinking that they must have picked up the wrong document, maybe for someone else. The sudden shock of a bucket of ice-cold water being thrown over me literally took my breath away; for a moment I was gasping for air, then pain seemed to explode in my brain as a hail of rubber truncheon blows rained down on me.

"No one asked when you were born," I heard the Commissar say from what seemed like a great distance. "We are telling you to sign and then we will leave you alone," the voice went on. I was released from the table and pulled upright, still standing naked in front of that table. The Commissar pointed to the document.

"Sign it," he repeated, sounding bored. I tried to read through swollen eyes and despite my blurred vision read that I freely agreed that what was written above was correct and agreed to be kept in prison for ten years. I signed.

When I returned to the barracks, Mother and Father and a few friends were waiting for me to help in any way they could with my cuts and bruises. I realised how particularly humiliating this must have been for the women, including my brave mother. It had become a pattern that whenever anyone returned from their interrogation, some of us would be there waiting for them to give them support after their ordeal. In normal times, these sadistic criminals would be locked away from society, but in war time, as history has repeatedly shown, they crawl out of some dark pit and find opportunities to commit their crimes with impunity.

During the months between the invasion of Poland and our arrest, the rest of the family had never known what Father had been doing or where he was. I took an opportunity to ask him and he told me some of what had happened.

"As you know we had orders to mobilise in August, I think it was the 23rd. I was with a cavalry regiment, it isn't safe to give you details, but I can tell you that after about a month of skirmishes, we found ourselves in woods south of Lublin, surrounded by the enemy. It was a lovely sunny day, but it rained in the night so everyone, Germans, and Poles, were stuck in the mud. It was stalemate. We managed to contact HQ in Warsaw but were told that they were in the process of dissolving. Rather than surrender, we decided to make a break for it and go north in the direction of the river Bug. We left the car bogged down in the mire, anyway it was useless to us in the terrain where we planned to travel, but we kept two of the horses. Within a few days we heard that Warsaw had capitulated so there was no point continuing to head in that direction. By this time the Soviets had occupied the eastern part of Poland and our soldiers in that area had orders to surrender. There was nothing for it but to go underground with the rest of the surviving Polish army, living sometimes in forests and sometimes in safe houses." He paused and I expected him to tell me about how he had been wounded in the leg, but he glossed over that as insignificant.

"I had been wounded as you know; I had to get it treated so took the risk of going home." He paused again, while some other memories seemed to pass over him unspoken. Then he continued, but detached, sounding more like a schoolteacher recounting history from books.

"Before the war, the Ministry of Communications had developed a very small radio receiver for intelligence. The factory had been occupied by the Germans, but our people were able to get some of the components and a couple of transceivers in working order. We needed to know the correct wavelength before we could use them. There were secret couriers who were in contact with the Polish consulate in Budapest, and they brought us information. Messages were all in code and the decipher people were all kept secret, so no one knew what the messages were." He stopped and looked at me.

"And like you Boy Scouts, we were only ever known by our nom de guerre. In our group we were held together by a special bond, like a brotherhood. We were conscious of living in a state of constant threat, that we were walking along a knife's edge, that every meeting could bring our final parting closer." His voice trailed away, and I left him to his thoughts and memories of the members of his brotherhood who he was never likely to meet again. But I felt privileged to have been allowed to share those memories, and determined to follow in his footsteps, one day fighting for a free Poland.

Father had already been interrogated early on in our incarceration, but in the early hours of one fateful morning he was dragged from his bunk, and I was taken too. The political Commissar was sitting at the big table and Father was told to stand facing him. I was made to stand in a corner; I guess I was there to add leverage on Father. The table had the usual instruments of torture laid out. The Commissar had a document on the table in front of him that he kept glancing at and touching, curling up one of the corners. He nodded to one of the prison guards and the standard treatment was meted out. Father was stripped and beaten but refused to sign the confession. It is one thing to have to endure such a thing, but quite another to watch helpless while someone you love suffers. Eventually the beatings stopped, and Father stood bloodied before the table again.

The Commissar picked up the document with which he had been so preoccupied.

"We know everything about you!" he almost screamed. He began reading from the document, "You were educated in St Petersburg. You were part of the Tsar's bodyguard. You were a cavalry officer in the Imperial Army. You were wounded and fled to Poland at the time of the Glorious Revolution. You fought against the glorious Red Army of Comrade Lenin and Comrade Stalin. You are a member of the Polish Intelligence. You have been a member of hit squads that have destroyed our steam locomotives; you have organised train crashes. You have been part of clearing areas of forest for hidden airports for Polish aircraft, and of clearing forest paths from west to east." He stopped for a moment and looked contemptuously at Father. I knew Father wouldn't have talked, but it seemed that somebody had; Father wouldn't have blamed them. The political Commissar continued in a lowered voice, using phrases that must have been standard issue for the NKVD.

"You are a rightist, a saboteur, a bourgeois nationalist, a counterrevolutionary engaged in espionage, a rat, traitor, spy, an enemy of the state, a persecutor of the working-class people. I will demonstrate to you our firmness, intransigence, and ruthlessness towards the enemies of the Soviet State and Party." This was said as a rising crescendo as Father stood tall and proud. "Order Number 485 may have been repealed, but as an officer of the Polish Army that we now know you to be, you are a category 1 prisoner for which there is only one sentence; sentences shall be carried out immediately." He took out a revolver and bang! He shot Father in the head.

The blood: it was terrible. I screamed and fell by my father. I grabbed at his coat and tried in desperation to cover him; I couldn't bear to see his head.

"Get off or we'll shoot you as well!" shouted one of the guards. I kept trying to cover him and hold him; somehow his legs were still moving although he was dead; it was terrible. After that, things became a blur. I remember people running and telling Mother,

"Your husband has been shot."

I remember that Mother was shouting and crying, lamenting inconsolably.

We were not allowed to see Father's body, and never knew whether he was buried properly or thrown out for the wolves to eat. I cannot bear to think of it now, even after all these years. I put my arm around Mother and told her,

"I will look after you; they won't kill you."

CHAPTER 15

ESCAPE (MARCH 1941)

Following Father's death, my interrogations were renewed. The interrogators would shout at me, trying to get me to tell them what Father had told me; what he had said.

"You bloodsucker! Capitalist!" they would shout as they hit me in the face with enough force to break my nose. They would kick me and treat me like an animal. I don't know how many times they broke my nose and how many times they kicked me. The fear of the pain was terrible, and I must admit that I frequently wet myself. I would ask myself, "Why don't they just shoot me and get it over with?"

"I don't know anything," I would tell them, "My Father told me nothing." At other times they would try to soften me up by offering me nice food.

"Just tell us the truth and you can have as much as you like." But I had nothing to tell, and the beatings would start again. I wished I could just die so that it would stop. I began to have recurring nightmares because of those interrogations; waking in terror to the sound of my own screaming.

In the early Spring of 1941, I decided that I had to escape. I knew it would be a long and dangerous journey and that I may not survive, but it was better than to stay where I was. My father had meant so much to me;

we had been such a close family. Somehow by losing my father I felt that I had lost my way. I knew Mother would need me but the urge to do something – to fight for my father was too strong. At first Mother didn't want me to go.

"I have lost Anna and your father and now you want me to lose you too. How can I live like this, without knowing if you or your sister are alive or dead?" she said with her face in her hands, as if she were praying.

"I have to try; to go and fight for my future – for our future, so that you have somewhere to go home to when all of this is over," I said, hoping that she could understand how I felt.

"How far do you think you will get? And on your own? You are still so young?" she asked.

"I'm going to ask Tomasz to come with me," I explained, "Two of us will have a much better chance than if I go on my own. I must try; if I stay here, I will likely die anyway." I hadn't yet spoken to Tomasz, but I was almost sure that he would be just as keen to try to escape. Now that I had made up my mind to it, I was filled with an exhilarating excitement and an intense impatience. At the earliest opportunity I shared my intention with Tomasz. I had already decided that the best place to tell of my plans would be while we were at our labour felling trees. That way I could use the cover of the general noise and chit chat. I had long since learned not to trust people under such intense stress as we were; our plans could so easily be betrayed even if unintentionally. The fewer people who knew of our plans the better.

"Tomasz, have you thought of trying to escape?" I asked without wasting time on any preamble.

"Of course," he said, "I think about it all the time, but not seriously. If it was at all possible, they would have proper guards and watch towers and barbed wire and such like."

"Just because they think it can't be done, doesn't mean that it is so, and maybe no one has tried before." I suggested. Realising that I was in earnest, he stopped working and looked carefully at me, his head tilted slightly on one side, as if he were trying to decide whether to continue the conversation. After a few moments, he nodded to himself, picked up his chopper and went back to work.

"I don't want to rot here like all those old Russian men," he said, "I'll come with you and escape this hell hole, even if I die trying, at least it will have been my choice." A few minutes later, he asked,

"Have you made any actual plans yet? Where we will be aiming for? Things like that?" Already we were a team and about to make our plans. We agreed to ask one of the children to sneak some paper and a pen out of school and made up a plausible excuse for this. We hoped that if we could get hold of a large enough piece of paper, I would be able to draw a map of Russia and its neighbours from memory. Map drawing had been on our curriculum at school and although I might not be any good at memorising and reciting poetry like Anna, I could remember maps.

It was a few days before we gratefully received some paper and a blunt pencil from one of the children. Tomasz managed to sharpen it a bit using the edge of one of the chopping tools although we were left with a kind of double point that drew two lines instead of one.

"It doesn't matter; look, I can still draw a map," I said happily demonstrating my geographic skills. I drew a rough outline of Russia as I remembered it and then added Poland.

"But we can't go back to Poland," objected Tomasz, "The Germans have occupied one side and the Russians are in the rest. What about trying to get to France; isn't that where the Polish government have gone?" he suggested. I couldn't add France to the map because I hadn't made Russia small enough and I needed to put Germany and Czechoslovakia in between.

"I think France would be too far," I said, "but maybe we could get to Budapest, Father told me there is a Polish Consulate there, but I still think it's too far."

"We can't go to China," said Tomasz starting to sound despondent, "Don't we have any allies?"

"The British government said they would support us, but we couldn't possibly get there," I said staring at the map. I tried to remember which countries were on the southern border of Russia and began to draw the Caspian Sea. I remembered that Iraq was southwest of the Caspian Sea. "The British Army is stationed in Iraq; if we could get to the Caspian Sea, we could probably get on a fishing boat or something and make our way south to Persia. I don't know if they are friendly but compared to our other options it looks like a short route across to Iraq from there," I suggested starting to feel positive that this was our best option. Since Tomasz didn't have a better alternative, we decided that we would aim, in the first instance for the Caspian Sea. "When we first arrived, we were somewhere near the Yenisei River, but then we travelled east. We can't ask about our location; it would be too risky; we'll just have to make a best guess." I said, thinking aloud. Tomasz dragged his finger along the map in a direct line from where we thought we might be to the Caspian Sea.

"If we followed that line, we would have to get right through central Russia; we could get arrested at any point, and it will be difficult to follow a south-westerly direction." I pointed to the map and dragged my finger along an L-shape route. "If we start by going directly south, which is easy to follow using the sun, we will come to the Russian border. Then we can turn west, again using the sun, and keep going till we hit the Caspian Sea. That close to the border is far less inhabited and I guess, if necessary, we could cross it," I said hoping that Tomasz would see the logic even if it might take longer. In the end that is what we decided to do.

Food was our next priority. We knew from the previous year that by May there would be wild berries for us to eat, but we didn't know much about what we might be able to eat further south or what to eat before the berries ripened. I thought that we would have to risk

86

asking locals about what we could eat and when, and asked Mother what she thought. Since she had already agreed to my going by then, albeit with misgivings, she offered to ask one of the Russian prisoners herself, who told us about the berries.

"How can they survive?" asked Mother.

"There are a lot of berries; the birds live on the berries. If you see the birds eating the berries, they are safe for you. The honeyberry is the first one, it fruits in May; you will find it growing on big bushes high up on the moors, by the rivers, in the forests and even by the swamps. They look like blueberries but are longer. The crowberries come later; they are black and grow low over stones and the red cranberries don't fruit till August, but they grow low on the stones as well," he said knowledgeably.

"But what can we eat in the meantime?" I asked, "If Tomasz and I dry and save half our rations for a couple of weeks that still won't last long enough." Mother thought our best chance was to let everyone in our hut know of our plans and ask them all to make a small contribution of bread to our venture.

When they heard about our plans, most people were shocked, saying,

"You will never get there," and "What? You are just children." They told us the wolves would get us or the police. But Mother encouraged me.

"If you escape, at least one member of our family will survive," she said. One of the other women tried to persuade Mother not to let me go, saying,

"Don't let him go; you'll never see him again; it's impossible. What will he eat? Where will he sleep? It's thousands of miles."

"Look, what can I do?" said Mother, "I can't hold him; he might die here; he might just as well die on the way to freedom." The woman turned to me then, imploring me not to do this.

"You are just a boy; you don't know what you are doing; you have no sense," then she appealed to those around her, "Someone talk to him." I knew she was genuinely concerned for my welfare but said with determination,

"Nobody can tell me what to do. I am going to fight because I want to fight for my father."

Some of the older men encouraged us boys to go and offered to teach us survival skills such as what to eat, how to sleep safely on the journey and how to cross the rivers. I had already learned most of this from my Scouting days in Poland, but we appreciated every little bit of encouragement and help. Most importantly they all gave us some of their food rations.

While we were saving up our rations, I also made myself a knife from the metal bands that were around the wooden barrels that were used as containers for the dried fish. I secretly spent many hours over many days sharpening this piece of metal; we were not allowed to have any sharp tools in case we attacked the guards. I had a good idea that I would need some sort of tool for getting food or maybe even to defend myself against predators; if the wolves attacked me, I would have something to fight with. I even managed to find a piece of wood and wrapped a strip of cloth around both tying them together to make a handle.

Some of our people were worried that the wolves would get us before we had made it very far, just as the guards had warned us when we first arrived at the camp. Tomasz was worried about the wolves too.

"If they attack us in a pack, we won't stand a chance," he said, "Can't we get hold of some weapons somehow?"

"If we get caught carrying weapons we'll be shot on the spot," I reminded him, "but if they catch us with nothing but some scraps of food, they'll just bring us back and we'll be no worse off." Tomasz saw the logic but was still understandably anxious about the wolves, and I must admit so was I. We asked one of the old Russians for advice. We found an ancient-looking short and wrinkled man who looked as if he might have some sort of wisdom of the ancients, although he was probably much younger than he looked because of the hard life.

"Have you ever been attacked by wolves?" I asked innocently, "and if so, how did you survive?" The old man peered at me, screwing up his eyes to try to get them to focus, and rubbed his wizened hand over his almost-toothless mouth.

"Wolves? Yes, I was chased when I was younger. People used to say that wolves are only scavengers and won't attack live humans, but I've seen different." His chin dropped and his eyes dimmed so that I thought that he had finished speaking, but he suddenly sat up and jabbed a finger at me.

"I blame Napoleon," he said, to my utter bewilderment, "In those Napoleonic wars there were thousands, no tens of thousands of dead soldiers just left lying in the forest, French and Russian. The wolves must have had a feast and got a taste for man-flesh. Then there were more wars and revolution and more wars and more dead bodies left lying in the forests. That's why the wolves attack us now." He paused and seemed to remember that I had asked him a question. "How do you survive a wolf attack? Simple, don't get caught. I'll tell you what you must do, you must sleep up in the trees; tie yourself on so you can't fall off in the night. As soon as you hear them howling in the distance, don't waste any time, get up into a tree and stay there until they're gone." He peered into my face again looking deep into my eyes as if he wanted to penetrate my inmost thoughts. "They are patient beasts; they can wait for days to see if you'll drop," he warned. He then announced that he was tired and didn't want to talk anymore and Tomasz and I left him alone.

"I just hope we don't meet any wolves where there aren't any trees," said Tomasz, accurately expressing my own thoughts, "and we need to make sure we find something to take with us to tie us on like he said."

Our next problem was to figure out how we would manage the actual escape. Since we were just a couple of insignificant boys, we presumed that we wouldn't really have to get too far away from the camp before anyone would be interested in trying to retrieve us; they certainly wouldn't bother sending out a search party and would doubtless be happy to leave us to the wolves. We really just needed to get out of gun-shot range and maybe half-a day away from the distance the guards might follow with the dogs.

"The guards won't let the dogs off their leads; they're too valuable, so they will only go as far as the men themselves are prepared to walk," I said, having frequently observed the lack of enthusiasm on the part of the guards regarding their guard duties.

"They're nearly always drunk by the afternoon anyway," said Tomasz disdainfully, "especially when they've just returned to camp with a fresh load of provisions."

"That gives me an idea," I said enthusiastically. "Look, they are nearly always friendly when they're drunk and happy to talk. When they go for supplies, they always take a few prisoners with them to help with loading the trucks. So, we wait for an opportunity when they're drunk and get them to tell us when their next trip will be. Then we can volunteer to help with the unloading of supplies, and when they are blind drunk, we can make our escape."

This looked like our best option, so that is what we planned to do. As soon as we found out the day of the next supply delivery, we began to collect all our stored food into sacks that we could tie on our backs under our outer coats. We said goodbye, hoping that it would be, and suffered all the ladies crying. I let Mother think that we would be going early the next morning, but we decided to go at the first opportunity under cover of dark; I couldn't face the parting and the inevitable tears.

In the evening of the day when the guards were returning with the supplies, friends helped us to strap our food sacks onto our backs as flat as they could get them. Then we put over-large coats on, for warmth as well as to cover our sacks and headed off to help with the unloading. As usual, the guards began to drink and naturally we encouraged them. Whilst unloading the supplies, we both took the opportunity to filch some extra bread and stuffed it wherever we could. There were other prisoners around who pretended not to notice what we were up to, thinking we had just come to pilfer some extra food.

It seemed to take forever for the guards to get well and truly drunk - enough for us to risk making our escape. The other prisoners had disappeared back to their barracks for their evening meal rations. We simply opened the gate and slipped though, shutting it behind us.

"Just walk," I whispered to Tomasz, "If we run, the dogs will hear it and alert the other guards. If the guards see us running, they will assume we are trying to escape and shoot; if we walk, they might think we are out here on legitimate business for long enough for us to get away." So, we walked, our footsteps softly crunching in the snow, not daring to look back. Slowly we walked away from the camp perimeter and into the woods.

CHAPTER 16

WOLVES (APRIL 1941)

We kept walking in silence until exhausted we slumped down against a tree to rest. The night-time temperatures were still below freezing in April, so we hugged together in our overlarge over coats, under which we had as many extra layers as we could manage, and hats pulled well down over our heads. There was no sight or sound of anyone trying to follow us, and I had lost sense of which direction we had been travelling. I knew I would have to try to get our bearings when it was daylight, and we took it in turns to sleep.

When I woke, I had a few panicky moments about being so far from any known point of reference, and in the cold light of day, I felt somewhat less confident than I had before. But I had no intention of letting Tomasz know. We sat silently nibbling some of our bread and scooped up mouthfuls of snow that was just beginning to show signs of a thaw. The snow melted into a refreshing drink in our mouths; it was a technique we had learned very early in camp. Thirst was something we had only occasionally experienced during the summer months.

"So, we are following the moss while we're in the woods and forest, right?" asked Tomasz, "I've heard about that before, and some of the old men mentioned it, but I've never tried it; does it actually work?"

"Well, most people just think that moss will always grow on the north side of a tree so you can work out your direction from that; but it's not that simple." I answered. "Yes, it does work, but you have to do it properly. I'd better explain it in case we get separated; in case you need to find your own way at some point in our journey."

"Okay, but I doubt that I would be able to get very far on my own; I expect I would give up and try to find somewhere to turn myself in. I never did like being alone," said Tomasz with worrying honesty. I got up and went over to a tree that conveniently happened to have some moss growing on it at the bottom of the trunk.

"Here is a perfect example of how you could get it wrong. What you need to remember is that moss grows where it can stay moist and wet. If you look at this moss, what do you think it will tell you?" I asked.

"Well, it seems to go all around, so that's no help," said Tomasz in evident confusion.

"Exactly; that's because the air is nearly always moist enough for moss to grow below about knee height. So, moss growing at that level can't tell you anything." We got ourselves ready to continue our travelling and I suggested that we continue to look for moss and hope that eventually we would find some that would actually help us get our bearings. I spotted some on an old, gnarled pine tree and beckoned Tomasz over.

"Look at this bark," I said, pointing to all the cracks and crevices, "you can see how the moss is growing in those bits which would collect water, so that's no help either."

"What about that one over there?" asked Tomasz hopefully. The tree that he had pointed out had moss growing along one of the side boughs. "It's above knee high and the bark is smooth-ish," he said hopefully.

"But we can't be sure that it hasn't just collected water there where it can't drain away, and it's not really on one side: it's more on the top. We need to look for straight trees like birch, with moss above knee height and obviously just on one side," I said hoping that we would eventually find something.

"What about the sun?" asked Tomasz, probably remembering some of the other advice we had been given.

"It won't work in amongst the trees; there are too many shadows, and the ground is too uneven. No, we'll keep looking for the moss; we're bound to find some soon." I said as we plodded on through the gradually diminishing snow. I wasn't too worried about exactly which direction we were going at this stage, just so as long as it wasn't north. My main concern was that the food that we had brought with us would last until we found berries and that would likely be sooner further south. But before we had found any convincing moss, we had our first encounter with wolves.

We heard the unmistakable howl of wolves in the distance at the same time and froze.

"Do you think they've picked up our scent; or maybe it's a deer or something," whispered Tomasz, not daring to speak aloud.

"There's no way of knowing. The safest thing is to assume it's us they're after. We need to find a tree that we can climb, and find it fast," I whispered back. It is remarkable how frustratingly difficult it is to find a tree suitable for two people to climb, that will also be high enough to escape a pack of wolves, when the tunnel-vision effect of fear sets in. Thankfully, once we had found such a tree, adrenaline gave us the strength to climb despite the numbing cold in our hands.

We could hear the terrifying howls of those wolves coming ever closer. The fear was paralysing; at each fresh, and ever closer, howl the adrenaline surged through my body like a tidal wave. With hands shaking, I pulled at the rag-rope that I had stored by wrapping it round me under my coat. I reminded Tomasz that we had been told to tie ourselves onto the tree.

"We need to tie ourselves on," I whispered at him, holding up my rope to show what I meant. This was not an easy task; my first attempt was useless as one end was hanging down and I hadn't managed to secure it to anything. I unravelled and started again, trying to think through the fog of fear.

"If we tie ourselves to smaller branches overhead it should work better," suggested Tomasz and I immediately saw the logic. Before we had finished, the lead wolf had reached the base of our tree. He put his head back and howled. Up close, the noise was terrific; I wanted to scream but somehow managed to keep it in. I could feel Tomasz shaking with fear beside me. We were about to find out just how high a wolf can jump.

Within minutes, the rest of the wolves had joined their leader; there must have been six or seven in the pack. We didn't even whisper and hardly dared to breath, let alone move, but those wolves could smell us; they knew we were there. They began jumping up at the tree trying to reach us, clawing at the bark. In their efforts to try to get to us they stripped the tree of most of its bark. They couldn't reach us, but they did not leave. Instead, they milled around the base of the tree waiting. Periodically a wolf would set up its terrifying howl as if trying to frighten us out of the tree or, becoming impatient, they would try yet again to claw their way up the tree to get at us. While they were there, we dare not eat and only slept fitfully by turns. The wolves stayed for three days before they eventually got tired of waiting and ran off. We didn't dare get down straight away, we waited several hours to be sure they had gone. By this time, we were in a bad way, having hardly eaten, unable to relieve ourselves properly, and utterly stiff from cold and immobility.

We were attacked by wolves in this way at least three times on our journey, and the memory of their terrific, frightening howls haunts me to this day.

Shortly after the first wolf attack, we finally found moss on a tree that we could rely on to indicate the north face. Although we had no point of reference at this stage, it felt to me as though we had been travelling in a roughly easterly direction. Standing by that tree we could see which way was south, but the wooded terrain didn't allow us to get a fix on a point far enough away to get our bearing for long. We would need to find another such tree or find a clearing so that I could use the shadow from the sun to guide us. It was at this point that I remember praying to Almighty God that we would choose the right direction and, trusting in His guidance, we continued on our way. We walked during the daylight hours and slept up on the branches of trees at night because of the wolves roaming the area. To be safe, we always tied ourselves to the branches so that we couldn't fall off in our sleep.

The worst physical obstacles that we encountered were the many very wide and fast-flowing rivers we had to cross. When we had to cross a river, we built a raft each from bundles of twigs. We needed a huge number of small branches and twigs to take our weight, and then we had to twist small twigs until we could make a sort of rope to tie the bundle together. Dry twigs were no good for this; they just snapped. We needed live branches that would bend; I was able to use my home-made knife for this job. Once we had made our rafts, we took off all our clothes and tied them to the back of our necks. Then we paddled the rafts with our hands, gradually pushing ourselves to the other side of the river. It usually took about a mile's length of the river before we got to the opposite bank of these fast-flowing rivers. When we reached the other side, we were blue and stiff from the cold. We would dress ourselves and then run around as fast as our strength would allow to try to get the circulation going and warm ourselves up.

We also had to cross vast expanses of moorland. On these open areas I was able to use the sun to guide our way. Tomasz hadn't experienced anything like the amount of Scouting training that I had done. His time had mostly been spent playing games and sitting around campfires, while I had been orienteering and learning survival techniques. I explained what I was doing the first time we had the opportunity to use the sun and shadows. I waited until roughly midday when the sun was at its highest as far as we could tell.

"Right, we need a long straight stick," I said scouring the ground for something to use. We had to break off a stick from a bush and it wasn't very straight. "It's not ideal, but it will have to do," I told Tomasz while I pushed it vertically into the ground. "Now we need to find something to mark the tip of the shadow," I continued whilst hunting around for a suitable item. I snapped off a short twig and pushed it into the ground. "Now we have to wait for the shadow to move about a hand width," I told him, and sat down while we waited. We had got to know each other very well over the weeks; he told me about his life on the farm and I told him about my life before our deportation. Sometimes we talked about things that we both remembered, like swimming in the Horyn, or fairs and other events in Rovno, or the gypsies in the woods. While we waited for the shadow to move, we just sat in a comfortable silence with our own thoughts.

"Now we can mark the new position of the tip," I said hunting for another short twig. Tomasz had already found one and silently passed it to me. "Right, now we draw a straight line between the two tips," I said drawing an imaginary line with my finger, extending it about a foot each side. Now, if I stand with my right foot at the first marker and my left foot at the second marker, I am facing south." I lifted my arm and pointed the way I was facing, "That direction is the way we have to go," I said with conviction.

By the time the food we had brought with us had run out, we were able to find plenty of berries. We ate anything we could find, but our main source of food was berries. When we had been back in the camp, we were told that if a bird eats berries from a bush, then they would be safe for us to eat. There was a huge variety of berries growing on bushes, and sometimes low on the ground or rocks, and so long as we saw the birds eating them, we did too. We stripped all the berries off the bushes and carried as many as we could. We put them in our shirts and everywhere we could to try to make them last until we found some more. Sometimes the berries were bitter, but if there was nothing else, we had to eat them. Because we had nothing solid or warm to eat, just berries, we suffered a lot from stomach pains and other gastric problems, losing a lot of weight and becoming very thin. Eventually we started to lose our energy and at times were very depressed by the endless journey.

After several weeks of crossing rivers and living on berries, Tomasz began to be unwell. He started coughing and he was bringing up phlegm; it reminded me of Anna when she had visited and been coughing so horribly. He tried to brush it off.

"It's just a cough; it couldn't be tuberculosis, we haven't been near another person for weeks and weeks, and no one in our barracks had it." That was true enough, but when his stomach upsets became worse and he began vomiting up what little we had eaten, I began to get really worried.

"I think we need to have a rest day," I said, knowing that it wasn't really an option, we had no choice; Tomasz couldn't continue in the state he was in.

We had just crossed yet another river and Tomasz couldn't seem to get warm again afterwards. I wrapped him in my overcoat and left him lying where I hoped any sunshine would help to warm him while I went to see what berries I could gather. There was a bush of blue elongated honeyberries, so I stuffed as many as I could inside my shirt and hurried back. Honeyberries are very sweet and nourishing, hence the name, so I was hoping that they would revive him, but he had no appetite and wouldn't eat. He just kept coughing.

After a few hours, while I wandered around aimlessly wondering what our best course of action was, he was showing signs of fever with chills and sweating. I noticed that his breathing had become very rapid and shallow.

"I can't breathe properly," he whimpered, "It feels like someone is sticking a knife into my chest if I take a deep breath." He began coughing again and cried out in pain, grabbing at his chest.

"Just keep taking little breaths then if it hurts," I said feeling utterly helpless and hoping that these pains would pass. More hours passed and then Tomasz began talking. At first, I thought he was trying to tell me something or remembering something about his life on the farm before all this had happened. But gradually I realised he was talking to someone else; it was someone from his family, but I couldn't tell who. He seemed to think he was back at home in his bed and kept asking why he couldn't go to school. Then he started telling someone to get off; to stop sitting on his chest. I tried to talk to him and tell him where he was, but he seemed to get even more confused when I did so, and I gave up.

There was no way I could get him safely up into a tree for the night, so I stayed there with him, desperately trying to stay awake and praying that tonight we would not be troubled by wolves. I must have dozed off because I remember waking in the early hours of the morning to find that Tomasz was no longer breathing. He had slipped quietly away; he was dead.

For a long time, I simply sat, numbly wondering what to do next. We had become very close over the weeks of our journey together and I felt as though I had lost a true friend. I felt bereft of all human contact – no family, no friends, not even any enemies – nothing.

Eventually, I carefully retrieved my coat from covering Tomasz and put it back on. Then I took his coat off so that I could cover him properly the way people do. I didn't want the wolves, or any other wild animals, to get at his body so I was determined to try to bury him. This was no easy task without proper tools. I began scratching the ground with sticks, but only manged to scrape out a hollow to lay the body in. The next best thing to a deep hole would be a pile of stones. I couldn't bear to put stones directly on top of him, so I found soft branches of shrubs to lay over him first. Then I piled as many rocks and stones over him as I could find, even dragging some up out of the river.

Most of the day had gone by the time I had finished. I hadn't stopped at midday to check our bearings after crossing the river, so I wasn't completely sure which way to head. I ate the honeyberries that I had collected for Tomasz, wondering why Tomasz had become ill and not me. What crime must I have committed to deserve such punishment? Why had Father had to die? Why had we been deported? Why was I here? I asked myself all the usual questions that people who have been bereaved ask themselves, with that unexplained and unwarranted sense of guilt.

"You chose this path," I heard my own voice replying. "You have the determination to do this. You must have the determination to do this, for Tomasz, for your sister, for your mother, for your father." I climbed up into a tree and tied myself in for the night as usual.

The next morning, I went back to the bush where I had found the honeyberries and stripped it clean. I waited for midday to determine the correct direction, then after a final check on Tomasz' grave, I sadly moved on.

CHAPTER 17

ALONE (SPRING 1941)

Travelling alone was much harder than I would have imagined. Any doubts that Tomasz and I had would have been stoically brushed off as we each sought to bolster the courage and determination of the other. But now, when I began to doubt that I would survive, I became very depressed. When I had a companion to share thoughts with, together we would notice things of interest or beauty as we journeyed, such as catching sight of a wild animal, or the view across the moors or valleys, or sunsets and sunrises, or maybe a cloud formation. But now I found I had little interest in what was around or before me unless it related to food or my direction of travel.

When I came to yet another river, I stood and began to contemplate the best place to cross. The water was clear and sparkling, bubbling over some boulders, and I caught a glimpse of fish well below the surface. I wondered if this river was a tributary that would be flowing into the Yenisei or even into the Lena; either way its destination would be the arctic where I presumed it would disappear under the ice.

"Why don't you just jump into that lovely clear water and give yourself some peace at last; wouldn't it be better to just finish yourself off?" I heard myself say. "Why bother to struggle on? You will fail in any case," the voice continued. The water looked appealing, and the thought of rest from the endless weariness, and now the unbearable loneliness, seemed such a simple solution.

"I would just slip quietly away; it would be easy," said a persuasive voice inside. But there was another voice in me; a voice of defiance, that answered.

"Do it tomorrow; that will be better than today. Just see what tomorrow brings." So, I decided to leave the difficult decision until the next day and made my way across. This happened to me time and again on the many occasions when I was faced with yet another river to cross. Many times, I thought of jumping into the water to drown all my weariness and take away the ever-present ache in my legs.

It wasn't just my legs that ached; I suffered from all sorts of aches and pains, headaches, and cramps, and digestive problems, from the poor diet, exhaustion, and stress.

"It's hopeless," I heard myself saying, "Why didn't I just lie down with Tomasz and let the cold put me to sleep."

"But the wolves might have got me first," I argued back stirring up some emotion to help spur me on. It was a persistent feeling of emptiness that I found hardest to try to overcome. Despite the fatigue, my sleep was fitful, never deep enough for real refreshment. Some days I seemed to walk for hours without a single thought and without any recollection of where I had been; like an automaton, just walking in the direction I had programmed myself to go with no other purpose to my existence.

I began to neglect myself, not caring about my health, other than trying to satisfy the unremitting gnawing pangs of hunger, and I stopped washing myself. Inevitably, I developed sores, and minor scratches and wounds quickly became infected. The lice that had for so long been my constant companion became more active as the temperature increased.

Much of Siberia is perma-frost: in the summer months it partly thaws, creating bogs. On this bogland, as I soon discovered, millions and millions of mosquitoes breed. At times, there were so many that the sky appeared black with them. They were an appalling nuisance, not just to me but also to the animals. I knew the only way to protect myself was to cover as much of my body as possible. These terrible insects get into your eyes, mouth, and hair looking for blood.

"You evil little bloodsuckers!" I shouted at them as I plastered myself with mud, coating every patch of unclothed skin. Looking back, I can only imagine what I must have looked like with just the whites of my eyes showing, but fortunately, I never met anyone in those areas of bogland. In the woodland and forests, even the reindeer were attacked by these insect plagues and would run into the bushes in an attempt to drive them away. Coming into one wooded area on the edge of this bogland, I decided to light a fire to try to keep them at bay while I rested.

"I need to light a fire," I told myself, "But I have no matches or tinder."

"But I have a knife," I argued with myself, "and if I can find some flint, I can make a spark."

"They will have sucked you dry before you find any flint," replied the pessimist.

"Then I'll use the stick and bow method," argued back the optimist, looking for a suitable stick and some dry brush to act as tinder. I managed to pull some threads from my clothing, enough to plait together into a strong string to loop around the stick for the bow. Much of the wooded areas were birch, but there were also pine trees interspersed so that at times I could use pine branches to create a lot of smoke; this was the most effective way to deal with the insects.

I walked as far as I could every day, going south all the time, without worrying about how many miles I had travelled, because my main priority was always finding food. Sooner or later, something turned up, but I always thought that it would be impossible to feel completely full. On one occasion I found a dead reindeer and another time a dead crow; those were the only times I found meat. My only dream was to have a really delicious hot meal and then to lie down and die.

Although I was not there as a tourist and my only aim was to survive, I was at times able to enjoy the marvellous scenery and the incredible vastness of Siberia. I have memories of beautiful and varied wildflowers, enormous flocks of birds migrating in the Spring to their nesting sites in warmer climes. I experienced the midnight sun that at times created a luminous almost phosphoric glow with a kind of twilight lasting through the night.

There were all kinds of small mammals and enormous herds of reindeer. The rivers themselves were absolutely wonderful to look at, wider than any I had seen in Europe.

The ground became more rolling and with a thicker growth of trees, the further south I travelled. I began to see fields of grass creating a sea of flowers, stretching far away on the horizon like a billowing ocean. In the distance I could see a lake stretching into the horizon. As I drew near, I saw the first men I had seen for months. There were two elderly gentlemen fishing at the water's edge. By this time I must have been in a terrible state, scratched all over and starving, with my long matted hair, like something frightening emerging from the undergrowth. Fortunately, because I could speak fluent Russian, I was able to explain straight away who I was and where I had come from, albeit with a voice dry and husky from lack of use.

"We know that many people try to escape," they said, "We know all about prisoners from the camp." They beckoned me over to them in a friendly manner, so I went over and sat looking hungrily at their fish.

"Are you hungry?" asked one of the men unnecessarily, to which I responded by vigorously nodding my head. They took their time, carefully filleting and then carefully cooking the fish on a flat piece of metal placed in the fire. They said not a word until I had been handed my fish, then finally one of them spoke.

"You must know that we are not allowed to help or cooperate with escaped prisoners," he said in a surprisingly

109

matter of fact way. "We will hide you in our hut, but you must be careful to stay hidden while you are with us, or we may be arrested ourselves." Again, I nodded in response whilst hungrily devouring my first taste of fresh fish. It was wonderful, and with it they gave me a form of flat barley bread, that they had baked over the open fire. I had truthfully not enjoyed such food since I had left my home in Poland. Despite the bread being covered in soot and dust from the fire, I ate every single crumb. But after having lived on little more than berries for so long, my stomach reacted badly to the fish, and I had terrible cramping pains. The men gave me some cold water and told me that I would live.

I was able to stay with the fishermen for a few days and continued to be fed on fresh fish. The sacking, the threads of which were still wrapped around my poor feet, was discarded when the fishermen kindly gave me a pair of felt boots – what luxury! They were hoping that in response to their generosity I would stay with them.

"The authorities demand a daily quota of fish that we must supply for the local store. With just the two of us, we are finding this difficult," one of the men explained.

"I can help you for a few days," I offered, "but I must try to find the Polish Army wherever they may be. From here might it perhaps be best to try to get through China?" I asked. The fishermen counselled me strongly against taking that route, so I stuck to my original plan to reach the Caspian Sea.

I was sad to leave the fishermen and their protection, but I was determined to go on. They told me the lake was called Baikal, so I decided that I had travelled far enough south and would need to take a westerly or south westerly direction from there. As I went west, the ground became more level, and I could see great flat stretches of grassland. After many more days, often with nothing to eat, I could see cows and sheep grazing together in pastureland and knew that I was approaching the inhabited part of Siberia. There were small lakes dotted all over where I saw ducks, geese, and other wild fowl. I began to see people in the distance – women doing their laundry in the rivers, fishermen and people working in the fields.

Eventually I came in sight of a small settlement. As I drew closer, I could see that the single-storey log houses, with high shuttered windows and fenced in yards, were much larger than I had anticipated from a distance. With some surprise, I saw that the richly coloured ornate Orthodox Church building was still standing in this tiny village. While still some distance away, I came across an elderly man who I later discovered was a shepherd. He had set up for himself a small camp site close to a small stream, from which he had presumably collected buckets of water. The man had made a fire and was busy boiling some meat. The delicious smell, to me who was starving and hadn't eaten anything warm for weeks, was almost overpowering. He spoke to me in Russian with an accent that I had not heard before.

"Are you hungry?" It was a rhetorical question; there was no doubt that he could see the hunger in my eyes. I nodded and crouched shyly nearby, like a wary bird coming for crumbs. His greasy plate looked as if it had already been used and I wondered momentarily if there was any meat left in the steaming pot. I wasn't disappointed; he spooned out some boiled meat still on the bone and passed it to me. I recognised it as lamb from the smell before I had even tasted it, almost drooling in anticipation. The meat was very greasy, and my stomach was no longer used to rich food having spent so many weeks living on berries and before that on dried bread and salted fish, and for so long on bread and soup. It tasted delicious, and I foolishly ate too much. The result was that I suffered terrible cramping pains that were so bad I thought it was going to kill me. The old shepherd was very distressed and stayed with me until I recovered, kindly giving me cups of fresh water from the stream. When the pains subsided, I thanked him for his generosity and told him that I had to continue my journey. I was more cautious about how and what I ate in the future.

As I travelled, I met people from different tribes who did not always understand Russian, sometimes only speaking their own languages, and sometimes speaking Russian with a local dialect that was hard for me to understand. Continuing further south, the terrain became more level, and settlements were visible from a distance. Seeing a few houses, close by the edge of a small lake, I decided to risk begging for food. I had no idea what I must have looked like to other people at that time; I was not yet old enough to need to shave so had no beard, but my thick black hair that was unwashed and matted had grown very long. Besides the grime, my face had been

112

darkened by so many weeks out in the open. The men who saw me approaching were busy working in a yard, loading a cart near a pile of logs. They stopped working and stood still, watching as I went towards them with the slow stride that I had developed over the months of walking. Two of them put their heads together, speaking in undertones, and I began to feel anxious. The need for food drove me on and I decided to take the risk.

Before I had a chance to ask if they spoke Russian, one of the men swooped behind me and locked me in an iron grip, both my arms pinned behind me and with both of his around me. He pushed me towards a small wooden building with a single-sloping roof that looked as if it was used for housing animals. He pushed me inside, shut the slatted wooden door behind me and locked it, putting a wooden bar across.

"What are you doing?" I called out in a panic, "Do you speak Russian? I only came to ask for food. Let me go." I couldn't understand why they had shut me in; I hadn't stolen anything from them, and they hadn't even given me a chance to ask for food. The men seemed to be discussing me, trying to decide who I might be and what my business was there. I overheard them mention the NKVD and was terrified that they were planning to hand me over to the authorities, thinking that they had somehow guessed I was an escaped prisoner. Eventually one of them spoke through the door.

"You are secret police; you are an NKVD spy." It was not a question but a statement, making clear that they had already decided what I was.

"No; you've got it all wrong," I began, "I have escaped from one of the prison camps."

"No one escapes," came the reply, "and how could you have travelled this far?"

"I have been walking for weeks and weeks," I said, "my friend didn't make it," I added, hoping that this might help to convince them.

"We don't believe you; you are a spy for the government; you want to take our food," one of them insisted.

"But I am only a boy," I said, "I am too young to be a spy."

"Then tell us why you are here." It sounded as if they might finally believe me.

"I have run out of food; I haven't found any berries or mushrooms in these woods. I came to beg you for some food, or at least to ask you to let me do some work to earn some food," I pleaded. Perhaps the argument about my age got through; fortunately, they eventually believed me and let me out. After showing me where I could wash, they took me to one of the women who gave me some food. It was lamb, but this time I ate only a small amount and slowly. Later, one of the men took me to a barn where he told me I could sleep. He was clearly still a little suspicious of me and didn't want me in the house.

"You can shelter in here and we will feed you until you have regained the strength to continue on your journey," he said with a hint of reluctance. Although they didn't want me sleeping in any of their houses, I was invited to join them for meals. The families in this remote village were just as curious about me as I was of them. They found it difficult to understand why my family had been deported from one country to a prison in another country so far away, especially as we were not criminals. They didn't know about the war going on in the west, about Germany invading Poland, or even about the Russians invading Poland.

"In the time of the Tsar," said one elderly man, "I travelled as far as the railway station at Krasnoyarsk. You had to cross the river Yenisei by ferry in those days; there was no bridge. I saw the trains coming from the west, bringing emigrants to come and farm here. Whole families came to work the land. But they weren't put in prison." He shook his head. "These Bolsheviks say their system is better for the people, but I don't know," he continued.

"Hush!" said one of the women. "Be careful what you say aloud; you know there are spies all over."

Under the socialising influence of living in a community again, seeing and speaking with other people, I began to regain my sense of self and to care about my own wellbeing and hygiene. Somehow when I was looking at other people, I became more aware of people looking at me and became more self-conscious in a healthy way.

The people in these settlements had a lot of meat from the animals in the forest, which they dried and stored for the winter months, but they were extremely short of bread and other food stuffs. It seemed to me that they lived a rather primitive life; their clothes and shoes were made of animal skins. They had no beds but slept on furs and moss on wooden slats. From the way they spoke and acted, I could see that they were themselves hiding from the Communist oppression and that was why they were so helpful to me once they had established that I was no danger to them.

Over the next few weeks, as I gradually regained my strength, I chopped wood for them in repayment for their kindness. By the time I left a few weeks later, I had chopped enough wood to last them for several months.

CHAPTER 18

CAPTIVE AGAIN (EARLY SUMMER 1941)

I walked for days and days getting more and more weary. I don't know how long because I lost all sense of time when covering the enormous distances between settlements. Every day it took all my determination to keep going. I had become aware that I was losing my vision and my teeth seemed to be going soft from the lack of vitamins and food. All my bones stuck out and I could count every rib; I was just skin and bones.

Eventually, I saw some men tending cattle and horses. After my last experience, of being held in such suspicion by the people of the village that I was locked in a shed, I decided to approach with more caution. I crept carefully towards them, hoping to remain unobserved whilst I tried to see what they were doing and who they were. As I watched, suddenly I was grabbed from behind by two powerful men. I hadn't heard them approaching and yelped in surprise and fear. I was aware that they were speaking to me but couldn't understand them.

The two men dragged me to their tent-like hut, lay me on the ground, tied my legs together and began to question me in a language that seemed to be part Russian, but the rest was unknown to me. I picked out a few words.

"...animals... stealing... thief..."

I tried speaking slowly in Russian, hoping they would at least understand part of what I said.

"I have not come to steal your animals; I have escaped from a prison camp in the north and am trying to reach the Caspian Sea." They seemed to understand enough of what I said but clearly did not want to believe me. Speaking in broken Russian, one man said accusingly,

"You come and steal our horses and cows. Men have done this before," he told me angrily. They left me tied up so that I couldn't escape whilst they went away, I guess to decide what to do with me. A short time later they came back and again began accusing me of being a thief; they were still convinced that I was after their cattle or horses.

"I am alone," I said, "how can I take you cattle or horses?"

"You have friends... in hiding," they accused but I sensed a hint of doubt in their voices. The irony struck me forcibly; how I wished I did have some friends.

"No, I am completely alone," I said. "I have walked alone for many weeks. I did have a companion when I first escaped but he did not survive the cold months. At another village the people let me stay and work for them so that I could have food and shelter." I read the continuing suspicion in their faces.

"Why are you in prison? You are thief!" They persisted in their belief that I must be a cattle thief.

"I was in the prison camp because I and my family are Polish," I tried to explain. There were shrugs and bewilderment all round. "Poland, my country, has been invaded and occupied by the Soviet Army," I said hoping for some response, but the blank looks continued. "The Communists deported my family and many others to Siberia," I tried again. This time there was something of a flicker of understanding in their eyes. Eventually, after several hours of questions, I managed to make them understand that I was Polish and trying to get to the Caspian Sea.

"Where is this Caspian Sea?" they asked, evidently unaware of the existence of the largest inland body of water on the planet. I pointed in the direction that I guessed it would be, judging by the last time I had taken my bearings. After some arguments between them, the questions stopped and they left me in peace – still with my legs tied together, while they prepared themselves a meal.

Hungry as I was, I had to sit and watch the meat being prepared and smell it cooking. At first, the men sat eating in front of me, making my mouth water excessively. One of the men, having finished with a bone discarded it near enough for me to reach. I grabbed it and started to gnaw at it like a hungry wild animal. The eldest man wrested it from me and threw it to the dogs, while I watched the animals enviously. But then the man handed me a whole piece of meat to myself, and I was allowed to partake of their meal. Perhaps they decided to feed me because I had not tried to escape; they may have reasoned that if I had tried to escape that would have proved I had been trying to steal one of their animals. They kept me tied up over night while they decided what to do with me.

The next morning, I was untied and taken to a small stream that was their source of water, where I was able to wash.

"You will work for us," said the man who had accompanied me, "You will work, and we give you food and somewhere to sleep." After a quick wash, the man took me to the fire that they kept going for their cooking. He didn't let me out of his sight. He pointed to the fire that had a very large cooking pot suspended over it, almost a cauldron of the sort you might read about in fairy tales.

"You will tend the fire and watch over the cooking pot," he said pointing at the pot. Then he took me to a pile of logs, and showing me the axe, said, "You chop wood." He then left me to it, but I was aware that I was kept under continual surveillance. At night, my captors, still highly suspicious of me, tied my legs together again. They did this every night, perhaps thinking that I might kill them in their sleep and make my escape.

The following day, after I had been let out and had my daily wash, the man took me back to the fire, but instead of cooking, I was told to boil their clothes.

"You will tend the fire and boil the clothes; to kill the fleas," were my instructions. He dumped a pile of clothes on the ground, then stood back to watch what I was doing. I began to hunt for a suitable pot to boil the clothes in. I rummaged around in all the nearby places while the man watched me in bemused silence. Having found nothing, I finally asked him to show me where it was.

"Where is the pot for boiling the clothes?" He pointed at the pot hanging over the fire.

"No," I said, speaking very slowly and pointing to the bundle on the ground, "for the clothes." Again, he pointed to the cooking pot hanging over the fire, and mimicking me slowly said,

"For the clothes."

The horror I felt at this suggestion, that I boil fleas in the same pot that we would eat out of, must have shown on my face because he put his head back and bellowed great guffaws of laughter. I have to admit that the food that I had whilst I was with these men was nevertheless wonderful, and I began to regain my strength. It was, like other food I had been offered, rich and greasy and upset my stomach until I had acclimatised to it. As the hunger faded and my strength returned, the incessant voice inside my head finally stopped telling me to kill myself, and despite being held captive, I began to feel more cheerful.

In the evening, one of the men handed me a fine-tooth comb and sat down in front of me. Presuming that he thought it was high time I combed out my long-matted hair, I set to it with little enthusiasm. It was nearly impossible to pull it through my hair that desperately needed cutting off. After waiting a few moments, the man turned around showing me an impatient face.

"No, you comb my hair," he said pointing to his own head. This was not something I had ever done before; Mother had always combed out Anna's long hair and then plaited it. My own hair had always been kept so short that it hardly needed more than a couple of fingers run through. I tried to pull the comb through the hair, but it kept snagging on tangles; each time this happened the man grumbled angrily. I picked up a small bunch of hair to make it easier and spied the head lice. Finally, it dawned on me that I was not supposed to be combing out tangles but lice! This became another one of my regular jobs, every night, combing out the head lice for all the men. At bedtime, they remained suspicious of me, and continued to tie my legs together for the night.

I wondered why there were no women in their camp who might have boiled their clothes and combed their hair for them. I gathered from their explanation that the women and children stayed in a permanent settlement somewhere whilst they herded the cattle to different pastures, I supposed a bit like shepherds. That explained the tent-like huts; their portable accommodation.

After a few weeks I felt stronger and started to plead with them to let me continue on my journey, but they always refused because by now I had become very useful to them. I decided to try a different tactic and stopped asking to be released. After a few days I began to talk about the future, including myself in the plans. I wanted them to believe that I had decided to stay with them permanently.

"If I am going to stay with you," I said after a short while, "then I shall need a place of my own." They looked pleased and agreed that a new hut should indeed be built for me. To help convince them of my intention to stay, I made suggestions on how to improve their own huts so that they would be more comfortable. I even showed them how to build a place to smoke their meat.

"Where I come from, in Poland, we smoke the best meat," I boasted, recalling fond memories of watching the meat being smoked and stored with the dried fruit in grandfather's barn. "It is best if you can hang the meat very high above the fire so that it hangs in cold smoke," I told them. Hardwood is considered best for smoking food and fortunately there was plenty of birch, which is a hardwood, in the region. I explained about the best wood to use and helped them with the construction. "The slower the process, and the colder the smoke, the better," I told them. "Smoke the meat for a few hours in the morning and again for a few hours in the evening and in between it can dry." The men were very pleased with this and began to be convinced that I no longer wanted to leave. They stopped tying me up at night. I just needed to patiently bide my time and wait for an opportunity to go.

We had started to build a hut for me when one of the men fell ill. He began to complain of a headache and went to lie down. When he didn't get up for his meal, explaining that he wasn't hungry, the others began to feel concerned. The headache didn't go away, and he began to complain of other aches and pains and tummy ache. The following day the man clearly had a high temperature and fever and had begun coughing. In their concern for him, the other men lost interest in me, especially as they had to share out his usual daily chores between the rest of them.

This was the opportunity I had been waiting for. I made myself wake up very early and watched them set off to milk the cows. Not knowing how long it would be before I found food again, I tucked whatever I could find into my shirt and wrapped some more in a skin that I bundled up like a bag. Then I slipped away. When I had first arrived, they had asked me about where I was headed, and since I had at that time pointed in the direction of the Caspian Sea, I decided to head off in the opposite direction in case they came after me. I knew this would be a long diversion to take, but I thought it would be safer.

I set off at a fast pace, not running, but walking with long quick strides to cover as much ground as I could without exhausting myself or creating a disturbance. I carried on in what I hoped was the same direction for a few days, but the weather was very cloudy, and I was unable to decide which way was north or south. I was trying by this time to follow a south westerly direction. Rather than continue in what might be the wrong way, I lay low and rested until the weather changed.

When the skies cleared, I could once again find my bearings and set off. The trouble was that the clear skies also left me a victim to direct sunshine, and on the open plains there was very little shade. After four or five days of walking in the open I began to hallucinate and imagined that I was seeing all sorts of things that turned out to be quite ordinary when I came up close. One day I imagined that I heard my mother calling me.

"What? How can that be? Can I hear Mother? Am I imagining?" I asked myself aloud, "I can hear a voice calling, but I can't see anyone." I stopped walking and strained my ears, trying to decide what, if anything, I really could hear. "Dogs!" I shouted to the wind, "I can hear dogs barking and where there are dogs there is a good chance there are people," I told myself and headed in the direction of the sounds. As I got closer, I could hear a cockerel crowing so I knew that I must be near to human habitation and soon came across a few well-constructed large log houses. This was, at last a sign of civilisation. The wooden houses had high steep roofs, with heavy cornices and ornamentation. They even had sash windows and wooden shutters.

Not wanting to be held captive yet again, I approached with caution but also with a nonchalant manner that I hoped would look innocent. Even so, I was again met with suspicion, but these people understood Russian, so we were able to communicate easily together. A man, who I took to be a kind of elder, asked the usual questions,

"Who are you, where have you come from, and where are you going?" The men of this small settlement carried hunting weapons and knives, so I felt inclined to give them a good explanation. I told them all the details, starting with the deportation from Poland, the death of my father in the Siberian prison camp, my escape with Tomasz and his subsequent death, and then my journey since then. I explained that I was trying to get to the Caspian Sea.

"If you can work for your food and shelter, you may stay until you are ready to continue your journey," said the elder. I was very thankful that, although they were clearly of eastern origin, they knew enough Russian for us to be able to talk together. I was shown a place where I could sleep, in a space next to the rest of one of the families and invited to join a meal. That first evening, after I had been well fed and had drunk hot tea from the enormous samovar, I was invited to tell them of my adventures as if I were a kind of guest speaker or storyteller.

"You have told us where you are headed, to the Caspian Sea," said the elder, "but you have not explained why."

"When the German army invaded my country, Poland, from the west" I began, "we put up a good fight. But a few weeks later we were betrayed by the Soviet Army who invaded us from the east. We could not fight on two fronts. Our independent Polish Republic had only been in existence for twenty years and we had not had time to build up a big enough defence force for that." The men listening nodded their heads sagely, as if perfectly understanding how that must have been. "Some of our soldiers surrendered to the German army and some surrendered to the Soviet army, but many managed to escape capture, and went to France to form an army to fight against the Germans," I continued. "The British government told us they would help, and I think they were helping the Polish government that went into exile. I remembered that the British had military forces stationed in the Middle East, so I planned to get to the British army by crossing the Caspian Sea."

"So, you do not yet know that Germany and Soviet Russia are at war?" asked the elder.

"What?" I asked, jumping up in surprise. "Ha! Perhaps they are receiving some of the medicine that they doled out to Poland!" I exclaimed. The elder didn't understand what I was saying, but understood that I seemed pleased, although perhaps he wasn't sure why. I sat down again and thought about what this might mean.

"Do you know anything about what is happening in Poland?" I asked hopefully.

"No. I know nothing of your country. We only know about the war with Germany because we have been warned that our people may be sent to fight against them," he said with a shrug of the shoulders. There was a great sadness in his eyes, and I wondered if he had been involved in the Civil War, the 1914 war, or the numerous smaller independence wars that had followed immediately afterwards.

"I wonder if I should change my plans and go back to Poland," I mused aloud.

"It would be dangerous to try to cross a war zone where battles will be raging, and you do not know if your country still has an army or even a government; they will not have had time to go back and may not be able to if it is still occupied," warned the elder. He was right; I would have to continue with my journey to the Caspian Sea and try to get to the British wherever they were. I still had a long distance to cover and hoped I had at least reached halfway by now.

I stayed with them for a few weeks to build up my strength once again, working hard for my food and shelter. But now I had the added anxiety of knowing that the Russian army was mobilising for war. There would be troop movements and doubtless the NKVD would be even more vigilant, on the lookout for German spies. One of the women kindly gave me some lightweight provisions for my journey and I set off once more.

The landscape had changed as I travelled south; in the early part of my journey the land had been covered by forests, marshes, and sandy wastes, and then as I drew nearer to Lake Baikal, this was interspersed with cultivable land and pasture. Once beyond the lake, the ground evidently became more fertile and there were fields and fields of wheat and rye, other cereals, and even what looked like potatoes. There were also vast expanses where herds of cattle, sheep and horses grazed. I was still having to cross large rivers and small streams and circumvent beautiful lakes of all sizes with clear, pure water. Every now and again I would catch a glimpse of the sun glinting on the gilded dome of a church in a distant settlement. The forests had disappeared, but there were scattered clumps of small birch trees. Wildflowers grew in the meadows with luxurious grass.

Before long I had resumed my diet of berries, and remembering the fresh fish, I found myself drawn towards the lakes, although I had no means of catching anything. There was one lake in particular where the tall rushes, that often grew around, seemed exceptionally tall. These rushes were like a jungle, tall and strong, in fact so tall that they were more like trees towering over me. The ground became swamp-like in places. The lake was fed by a river and on the river side I came across an elderly fisherman, sitting next to an old hut. He knew very little Russian, and I don't think he cared much for the Russian people either, but he was willing to share some of his fish with me. I nibbled my portion slowly in anticipation of the inevitable cramps that would follow.

It was a strange and remote place, and I was curious about it. I wanted to know what kinds of wildlife lived in this jungle of reeds, and with many hand gestures, I think he understood the question. Of course, I may well have misunderstood, but I thought he was telling me that along with the usual wild fowl such as ducks and geese, and horses, there were wild boar, wolves, and tigers! Not wishing another encounter with wolves, let alone tigers, I departed and in future avoided any areas of marshland where reeds were growing.

The felt boots I had been given, although comfortable, were at times too hot. Partly to preserve them and partly to cool down, I frequently went barefoot. The souls of my feet became tough and leathery. The seemingly endless flat plains, often with few points of reference, felt like an interminable obstacle to overcome. There were times when I went for days without any food. The physical and mental exhaustion caused me, yet again, to hallucinate. My doubts of survival resurfaced, and the lack of food and anxiety caused me to imagine all sorts of strange things. At one time I started to hear music; it was very clear and sounded like a large military band like the ones that I used to listen to at home. Another time I heard my mother's voice telling me what to do, and I even imagined I was back at school, working on a project, or that I was with friends in the Boy Scouts preparing to go on camp. I quite clearly saw cathedrals and large churches in the distance.

These visions, hallucinations, were always in the evenings, perhaps because of the half-light of dusk. Sometimes they were pleasant, such as when I heard Mother talking to me, encouraging me on, or when I heard beautiful music and saw churches. But at other times, they were absolutely terrifying. I saw the tragedy of war flashing before my eyes; the bloodshed and everything horrible that it was possible to imagine. As quickly as these hallucinations came, they suddenly vanished, and I became confused as to whether I had really seen something or imagined it. I prayed every night and every day. There was no on else to help me, only Almighty God; nothing else mattered.

I was now passing through farmland and pastures, the weather was increasingly warm, and I began to find more food, either from the fields or given to me by kindly people. It was often fifty or a hundred miles between villages; I kept thinking that I would never come to the end of it all. Now that the country was mobilising for war with Germany, the shortages that the population had already been suffering increased. Occasionally I was able to talk to people on the road and they told me the various rumours that were spreading all over the country. The Government were not sharing information about the war with the general public, they were simply told to double their efforts and work together to fight the Germans in their patriotic war. The majority of people seemed to rely on rumour to know what the state of the war was.

People I encountered were still suspicious of me because I looked so ragged and skinny, but I think the fact that I was a youngster saved me from being taken as a spy. Whenever I stayed anywhere, for even a few days, I would usually be told by the village elder to leave as quickly as possible. They were very anxious that they might get into trouble for helping a stranger. I made a habit of skirting around the larger villages, to avoid the possibility of being picked up either by police, NKVD, or military personnel.

Sometimes I saw a train, miles from any kind of settlement, just standing on the railway lines in the middle of a field. I didn't know why they were there or for how long they would stay. Twice I managed to hitch a lift on a train. The first time, I realised that I had been going in the wrong direction, and it took me several days to regain lost ground. The second time was very successful, and I managed to ride in a goods train for maybe three or four hundred miles. How different from the train journey the previous year. This time I was able to see something of the terrain through which I was travelling. There were odd little buildings following the line of the railway track at regular intervals. The freight train stopped next to wooden platforms, that I guess were sort of goods stations, where sacks of grain were loaded on. Looking southward from the train the land just seemed to stretch into the distance, a wild flat ocean of grasses.

There were many occasions when I was able to hitch a lift on a goods lorry, but the drivers usually expected a tip, and when I told them I had no money, they were quick to drop me off. I never stopped trying; hitching a lift felt like a sort of last hope to try and cover the interminable distances.

I found myself getting fond of the ordinary Russian people, the farmers, the shepherds, the herdsmen, and even the lorry drivers. Secretly I hoped that the German invasion would destroy the oppressive Communist system. I thought that Russian people were nervous and suspicious of everyone; they had no freedom and did not dare to criticise the authorities. In fact, it seemed to me as if the whole country was more or less a giant prison camp. The people I met were terrified to discuss their conditions in case they were overheard and denounced as a traitor. They knew that would have meant either instant elimination

132

or imprisonment in northern Siberia where they would likely have perished.

CHAPTER 19

A WEDDING (MID-SUMMER 1941)

After some time, I would guess around the middle of summer, having walked through miles and miles of pastureland, I came upon a small community of nomadic people living in tents. The tents, of a style that I had seen from time to time on the distant plains, were round with a dome-shaped roof. There were some boys tending cattle, horses, and sheep, and even a few camels, in the fields nearby. There were some women near the tents who saw me approaching. Judging by their reaction, they were clearly frightened by my appearance. My legs by this time had become so weak that I was using a stick to help me walk and my hair was once again a long matted unkempt mass of thick black tangles, and I must have looked very much like a wild animal, for that is how they treated me. They called for one of their men to come and deal with me. Fortunately for me, the men could speak some Russian, possibly because they needed to conduct trade with the locals, so I was able to ask for food and shelter. They agreed to take me in and feed me.

I was still clothed in the sacking from the prison camp and had gone for some time without washing. The children were kept well away from me and they put me in a sort of quarantine, probably in case I had any diseases. The man showed me where I could sleep, outside with the dogs and he handed me some animal skins to sleep on.

"You can sleep here until we can civilise you," said the man, "I will bring you food; the dogs will keep you company."

Thankfully the dogs, who very quickly recognised that I was no threat, were very friendly towards me. But for me, in that moment, more important than the friendliness of the dogs, was that they gave me as much food and drink as I wanted.

One of the women brought the food out to me; following in her wake was a train of curious children wanting to have a look at the stranger, who she shooed away. The woman put a wooden tray in front of me laden with bread, eggs, meat, and cheese and what looked like a jug of milk.

"Eat!" she commanded, waving the dogs away from me.

I was to discover that this was their staple diet, other than the bread it was all from their own animals. These were mostly rich foods that I was no longer accustomed to. The drink they gave me, that tasted like watered-down sour milk was also rich and fatty. I knew I had to start with small meals, as my stomach would not manage to take as much as I thought I could eat. Even after having taken precautions, I still suffered acute stomach pain after eating.

In the morning, they found me bent double and grovelling on the ground in agony, clutching at my abdomen. One of the women saw that I was ill and hurried back into her tent. She returned a short while later carrying a bowl and spoon with some sort of liquid in it that she had prepared for me. Writhing in agony, I wouldn't keep still enough for her to administer it to me. She handed the bowl to one of the men with an impatient gesture. He took me in a vice-like grip and forced the foul-tasting potion down my throat. The taste was absolutely horrible, and I can remember the taste to this day. I found out later that it was made from the urine of horses! But I did recover.

When I was back on my feet and my stomach had resumed some normality, they told me I would have to work for the food I had eaten.

"We all work," said one of the men, "you will work in the fields with the animals. The other boys will show you what to do and the dogs will help."

As well as their domestic chores, the women worked dying wool and weaving. They wove carpets and rugs; they worked mainly inside the tents, but the larger carpets were woven outside under a temporary canopy with old covers laid on the ground to protect the new work. They had a kind of loom with two poles and a huge heavy comb that they used to drive the pile together. The young girls helped with this, seated in a row on the ground. They didn't appear to be working from any pattern, just from memory. I was interested in the machinery and how they were operating it and went to have a look; the girls fell into a fit of giggles and couldn't work in front of me so I left them to it.

The round tents were made with a thick course felt, presumably made from the wool of their sheep and goats. Eventually, I was trusted enough to be cleaned up and allowed inside. My hair was cut by one of the men; I guess they were still cautious about allowing me into too close contact with their families. My sacking clothes were taken away and destroyed. I was given some old clothes for working with the animals, and I was given new clothes to wear when not working; I must have looked quite respectable by then. One of the women pointed to her family tent.

"Come," she said encouragingly, "you can come inside now."

As I passed through the opening, I was stunned by the sudden colour of the interior. It is difficult to imagine anything richer and more vibrant. The floor was covered with carpets and rugs with intricate designs. The walls were encircled with hangings and tapestries. It made me think of the account of the Tabernacle in Exodus when the Israelites were wandering in the wilderness and had to build a tent for the Ark of the Covenant to take with them. I stood on the threshold in awe and amazement, and the woman seemed pleased with my evident admiration of her work.

"We sell these to merchants for good money," she said with understandable pride. Inside I was invited to sit with the family and enjoyed what for me was a veritable feast. We sat cross legged on the floor and ate with our hands. All the while the children stared at the stranger in their midst and asked questions about me. The Russian-speaking adults translated for me, but I found this quite exhausting after having become so used to my own company and not having to make conversation.

After a few weeks of good food, rest, and secure shelter, I began to feel healthier and fitter, I also became more cheerful and willing to talk. I explained who I was and told them all the stories of my adventures since my escape; I didn't want to remember the prison camp, but I was happy to talk of my home in Poland. They could hardly believe that I had survived such an ordeal.

"You must be a very brave man," said one of the women.

"I'm not a man yet," I told her laughing, "and I think some would say foolhardy rather than brave."

Over the next few weeks, I worked alongside the other boys mainly in the fields watching over the animals, making sure none of them wandered too far away and helping with rounding up when necessary or fetching buckets of water for the trough. It wasn't easy trying to communicate because their mother tongue was nothing like Russian; we tended to grunt and gesture at each other. But I did make friends with one of the dogs. He took to following me around and it was a comfort to feel his friendship, the touch of his whip-like tail, and his inquisitive wet nose.

Now that they considered me to be civilised, I slept with the other boys, all of us in a row in one of the tents. Very quickly I found myself getting used to this life; I thought that it would do me good to stay a few months to really regain my strength for the next leg of my journey. I dreaded the thought of having to go back to not knowing where my next meal was coming from or where, or even if, I would find somewhere to shelter and sleep overnight.

One evening, at mealtime, I noticed one of the young girls smiling at me in a curious way and wondered what was going on. After their initial interest, most of the members of the families had continued to keep their distance and generally ignored my presence except when there was work to be done. The conversation around me was all in their own language so I had no idea what they were talking about or if it involved me in any way.

Shortly after this, one of the men approached me and explained in Russian that the families had decided amongst themselves that it would be useful to them if I stayed. That was fine with me, I had been hoping to stay for a few months anyway. But then he dropped the bombshell.

"You will marry one of our daughters," he said. It was not a question but a statement of intent; I clearly had no say in the matter.

"What? You must be joking!" I said disbelievingly. I really did think they were joking. One of the older women came and joined in the conversation.

"Look," she said, "We are short of men; she needs to get married. There are not enough men; you will marry her," she explained as if a wedding was an everyday occurrence; just another regular chore.

"I am too young to marry." I objected.

"For our people and customs, you are old enough," came the reply. I still thought they must be joking so said no more. But the next day, the man spoke to me again.

"In our tradition, the groom must pay a bride price to the family to win his bride, but we know you have nothing," he said, hunting for the correct words. 'That settles it' I thought, I can't afford a bride even if I wanted one, which I don't.

"But we will allow you to win her by demonstrating your prowess on horseback; this is also a tradition," he continued, "we call it Kok-boru. In Russian this means 'blue wolf' because we must protect our herds and flocks from wolves." I had no idea what this task involved, but the mention of wolves was enough to make me recoil in dread. "You will work an agreed number of years for your father-in-law to pay the bride price," he added with devastating effect.

It finally dawned on me that they were in earnest and expected me to marry this girl. I viewed the prospect of marriage with one of their daughters with horror and tried once again to object.

"But I can't marry anyone; in our tradition, from my home in Poland, I am too young."

"If you find you do not like her, you may easily divorce her later," he told me and walked away. I was appalled by his answer, not least because my family and I are devout Roman Catholics and have very strong beliefs about divorce. There had been no mention of timescale so I began to hope that they perhaps had some distant date in mind when I would already be long gone.

However, a couple of days later, as I was returning from work in the fields with the other boys, I could hear singing and music playing, along with the distinct rhythmic sound of drumming.

"What is it?" I asked, "What's happening?"

"There will be a wedding," said one of the older boys who knew some Russian.

"Who is the lady?" I asked, hoping it was one of the older women who would be getting married to an older man. He pointed at the girl who had been smiling at me, who was standing near the tent in her long swinging skirt that reached to the floor.

"That girl," he said.

"Who is she going to marry?" I asked, anticipating the answer.

"You," came the unwelcome answer. "There will be three days of celebration," he added with evident relish. Later that evening, I was taken by one of the older women to where a new tent had already been prepared for us.

"You will be able to sleep here with your bride," I was told. "There will be a rolled-up carpet between you so that you cannot touch each other. You can get used to each other; this is our tradition."

One of the younger women proudly showed me the clothes that we would wear for the ceremony. She held up two robes that had been exquisitely embroidered around the neckline, sleeves, and along the hem at the bottom. Then she held up a tall conical hat, also embroidered and with a long veil attached at the apex.

"This is for the bride," she said holding it up for me to admire. I grimaced, trying not to offend her. Then she held up another hat of matching fabric with one of the robes. It was a curious shape, about the size of a flowerpot but with flat sides so that if you looked from the top, it would have been sort of diamond shaped, and it had an upturned rim.

"This is for you to wear," she said with a toothless grin. Somehow, I still couldn't believe this was really happening and wondered if things had got lost in translation and it wasn't me that was supposed to be getting married at all but someone else. After all, there had been other times when there had been confusion between the two languages.

But the next day, when we returned from working in the fields, one of the women came for me and took me to the new tent and enthusiastically showed me where two beds had been made on the floor.

"That will be your place," she said, nodding.

"My place?" I asked, hoping once again that I had got it all wrong.

"And that's for your wife," she said, confirming that I was indeed the intended groom. Outside, the celebration had already started. There was dancing and music and feasting, but for me this was horrible. When the celebrating was over, we were taken to our new tent, and each lay in our separate beds with the rolled-up carpet between us. All the time I was wondering how I could get away from this.

I lay down and tried to go to sleep, intensely aware of the girl lying nearby. Suddenly I was startled as she reached across and patted me. I looked up to see what she wanted, and she smiled very sweetly at me. I pushed her hand away.

"Go to sleep," I told her. The next moment I felt her putting her arms around me. "Get off," I said, "Go away." When she persisted, I couldn't stand it. I got up, went out of the tent, and ran over to the trees.

"This is not my wife," I told myself, "I don't want to think about wives and being married. I'd rather sleep out here." The girl, my so-called wife, must have been upset because I could hear voices and crying.

"Don't worry," I heard them say in Russian knowing that I could hear them, "He will come back." It was no hardship for me to sleep outside; I did not go back inside the tent.

In the morning I was still hiding in the bushes, but they sent the dog after me. I could hear them shouting and calling for me. The dog that I had befriended soon found me out.

"What are you doing here?" they asked.

"Looking for something. I don't know," I muttered unconvincingly. They took me back, laughing at my

143

reluctance to face my bride. But I was determined to go before the roll of carpet could be moved and set about planning how to get away.

Very early the next morning, before anyone else had a chance to stir, I got up and went to the food store. I ate as much food as I could possibly manage, then I hid as much cooked meat as I could around my body, tucked inside my clothes; it was mainly horsemeat. When I was given my chores for the day, I set off as though going to work as usual. One of the regular jobs was looking for animals that had strayed; they were always losing animals, and somebody had to go and find them with the dogs. I pretended that I was going to look for some stray sheep. As soon as I was out of sight, I ran off as quickly as I could.

The dog that had befriended me and had got used to spending the day with me, trotted after me. I hid in some bushes and after a while I could hear voices shouting as they tried to find me. The dogs were barking, and I was terrified that my dog would follow me and start barking and give me away. I had become very fond of the animal, but I was so desperate to get away that I even contemplated having to kill him, but to my great relief he finally got the message and went back to the settlement, and I was at last able to escape. It was very disappointing; I had really hoped that I could have stayed for longer. Instead, I was back on the road, facing the unknown, but determined to reach my goal.

Travelling was much easier now that I had some fairly respectable clothing and my hair had been cut and washed.

People that I encountered on the roads were far less suspicious of me and evidently didn't feel the need to give me such a wide birth. Because I had a few days' supply of cooked meat, I was able to look around and appreciate some of the landscape rather than focusing only on looking out for something to eat. The land was now almost completely flat, stretching all the way to the horizon in all directions. The mid-summer weather was very warm and mostly pleasant, and the rivers and streams, where I could refresh myself, were plentiful, criss-crossing the black fertile plains. My journey southwest continued.

CHAPTER 20

THE KOLKHOZ (LATE SUMMER 1941)

The next break in my journey occurred when I had stopped for a drink and a rest by one of the many rivers. Not far away there was a village settlement and what appeared to be a large collective farm. I could hear a lot of laughter and the sound of female voices chattering and giggling. As I glanced across to see where the disturbance was coming from, I was surprised to see a crowd of women and girls coming from the direction of the farm buildings and running straight towards the river. Reaching the riverbank just a short distance away from me, I realised to my dismay that they were stripping off for a swim. They all stripped off, totally unselfconscious, and jumped naked into the water, swimming and splashing playfully, whilst I averted my eyes in embarrassment.

It wasn't long before they spotted me and wanted me to join them.

"Come on in," shouted one of the girls. I was far too shy to swim with a crowd of naked women.

"I can't swim in deep water," I protested hoping they would leave me alone. Howling with laughter, a group of them reached out and grabbed hold of me and pulled me, still fully clothed, into the water. Unable to defend myself, because they were women, I had to endure the humiliation of having soap rubbed onto my face and into my hair as they gave me a thorough wash and clean up. When they had finished the washing, I was able to climb out onto the bank and dry out. After the ladies had dried and dressed themselves, one of the older women, a pleasant middle-aged woman, kindly combed my hair into some sort of order, pulling out pieces of straw that had become tangled in my thick black hair.

"You look as if you've been sleeping in a haystack," she said.

"That's exactly where I have been sleeping," I said, "It's very comfortable sleeping outside in this weather."

"When did you last eat?" the woman asked in a kindly tone that hinted at an offer of food.

"A couple of days ago," I said, "but I have had plenty of water to drink at the river."

"Look, you don't have to tell me where you come from, or even where you are heading," she said, "but I can offer you food and lodging if you are interested. My husband is away; he is fighting a war with the army, and I have many jobs that need attention. There is a room in my house where you can stay if you are prepared to work." I wasn't very keen to go with her, but she was right that I needed food and rest.

"Come and stay with our Tanya," said one of the younger women, "or you might die of starvation before you get another offer as good as this one," she added laughing. The women treated me with motherly kindness, so I agreed to stay and work for a few weeks.

My landlady, Tanya, had plenty of work for me. In the garden I had to mend the fence and repair garden tools, and I painted the inside of the house with lime wash. When I had finished the painting, she pointed to her stone-built fireplace that had half collapsed.

"Can you repair that?" she asked hopefully.

"I can have a go," I offered, "it's inside so whatever is used to hold the stones together doesn't need to be waterproof." Tanya was happy for me to have a go even though I told her I had no experience of doing that kind of work. I was able to use the existing stones and mixed up a kind of mortar using sand from the riverbed mixed with some earth and added some straw – I thought perhaps I had seen people building their houses that way in Poland. I felt quite proud of the finished work. Tanya's neighbours were all very interested in what I was doing, apparently thinking that I was practical and innovative. Many of them wanted me to do odd jobs for them too.

"You can see for yourself," Tanya told me, "The village is full of women and children; the only men left here are very old. We must all work in the kolkhoz, and we have very strict quotas to produce, but the machinery and tools are very neglected." It was clearly impossible for these women to get help from anyone else, so I was able to be very useful to them in return for my board and lodging. The ladies came to me for all sorts of advice. On one dreadful occasion a desperate woman came to me clutching a baby in her arms. I found the poor infant's heart-rending cries very distressing to hear, especially as I was utterly unable to help.

"My baby is very ill," she sobbed, "and no one knows what is wrong."

"I'm not a doctor," I told her, "I have no medical training or experience, and I'm too young to have children of my own."

"You know more than I do," she said, pleading, "You might be able to help." She was convinced that I could help no matter how much I tried to impress on her that I was neither doctor nor nurse and knew nothing about illness.

There were no medical facilities in the community, and the women complained that they had to work regardless of their state of health. Another time an elderly man brought me his wooden leg.

"It's broken," he said, holding the wooden stump in front of me, "I can't wear it; I can't get about without it," he added and looked up at me with trusting eyes, convinced that I could save him from his immobility. Fortunately, I was able to find some good wood to use for replacing the broken section, and had enough skill to make the repair, and he was able to wear it again. While I worked on his wooden leg, the old man talked about the old days before the Bolsheviks had taken over all the farming communities.

"We were very prosperous here in the days of the Tsar," he said. "We farmers all had several horses and many cows. You see this black earth? We can grow anything in it without needing manure or fertilizer. We grew the biggest cucumbers in the world," he boasted holding his hands up to show me how big, just as a fisherman might boast of his catch. "Now the State takes everything we grow, and we don't want to dig up our potatoes just to give them all away, so we let them freeze in the ground in winter," he continued sadly.

I soon learned that the women were sent out to distant meadows to collect the harvest, raking hay, or digging up potatoes or other root vegetables the whole day. Because of the shortage of men, some of the women had to do hard manual labour such as digging water ditches for irrigating the fields. There was also the milking to be done two or three times a day. Mealtimes, unlike those I had enjoyed with the nomad community, consisted mainly of the ubiquitous black bread and thin vegetable or potato soup, and some of the produce from the dairy. One of the younger girls, her curiosity piqued, asked me where I had come from and what kind of food I was used to. I knew that the Russians were now at war with Germany but had no idea in what position the Poles now stood in relation to the Russians. I hadn't seen any obvious signs of NKVD influence in the community so decided to risk telling her that Poland was my home country.

"My family is from Poland," I said, "At home we had the most delicious fruit with giant pears that tasted of honey…"

"My grandparents came from Poland," she interrupted, "they were Catholics. Tell me what it is like there."

"I can't tell you what it is like now," I said, "but I can tell you what it was like before I left – before the invasion and war." So I told her about the town and the fairs and the river Horyn, but left out any details

150

about my family — that subject was far too raw to talk about.

It wasn't long before the manager of the collective farm, known as the Chairman, had heard about me. I guess he was interested to know what sort of person I was and what my plans or intentions might be. He had something of the Cossack look about him, but his features were too coarse, and he gave the impression of being rather slow witted. He took me to visit the farm.

"You can see that we only have women and children working here," he said, "the old men are no good — if they were they would be in uniform fighting in the army. I need some help with work that the women cannot do or have not the skill or strength to do."

"What kind of jobs do you mean?" I asked warily.

"There are many repairs to be done; I am told you are good at this," he told me bluntly.

"I am willing to repair things if I can," I told him, "So long as I can still continue to help the ladies when they need it." The first of my tasks at the farm was to repair a milk churn. When the Chairman was satisfied that I could be trusted to do the work, he took me to a tractor that needed servicing.

"Can you get the tractor working again?" he asked hopefully.

"I have not had anything to do with tractors before," I admitted, "but most vehicles just need basic maintenance to keep them going. I'll do my best," I promised. I set about cleaning everything I could and tightening up all the loose screws and bolts. It was a great relief when I was able to get the engine to start up. The Chairman was evidently pleased with the result and offered me more work.

"I will get you some official papers and register you as a farm worker so that you can continue to work here and maintain the machinery," he offered. Seeing this as a good opportunity to earn my food and keep, while rebuilding my strength, I agreed to it although I warned him that it could only be a temporary arrangement.

As soon as I felt stronger and fit enough, I told Tanya that I would shortly be continuing my journey south.

"Viktor, you must know that the Chairman is not a nice man. He will be good to you because you are a boy, but to us women, especially the younger ones, he is very bad," Tanya told me. "Let me come with you; I would like to move further south to get away from this man," she implored. I thought about the lime-washed house she lived in with its fireplace and a bedroom; the clean fresh river nearby and the availability of food and work, and I thought about the other settlements I had seen on my journey.

"You don't know how lucky you are," I told her. "This man may abuse you and cause you trouble, but at least you have good accommodation and work here. If you move south, you will still have to work hard; there are shortages everywhere; I have seen it. There are many settlements where people have harder work with less food and terrible accommodation, and you cannot be sure that you will not have to face another such man or even worse – I have seen terrible things," I finished, choking on the memories. She seemed to accept what I was saying and heeded my warning.

Tanya wanted to show her gratitude for the help I had given her; she and the other women gathered together some better clothing for me and cut my hair again. Then, after collecting a stock of provisions together for me to carry with me, and feeling far more human than I had in a long time, I cheerfully set off once more, waving goodbye to a sea of tearful faces.

By now, the late summer weather was very hot, and I was able to sleep in haystacks and other such places. It was warm enough to sleep outdoors without any discomfort, and the warmth meant that I did not get so hungry during the day and was able to make my provisions last longer than I had expected. I slept very well in the cool of the open air and the comfort of the soft grasses inside the haystacks. After one such really good night's sleep, having slept much longer than usual, I was woken by a strange sound; I heard a swishing noise not too far away from me. I lifted my head, and blinking bleary eyes, peered sleepily through the hay to see what was making the noise, expecting to see some sort of animal, maybe some cattle swishing their tails. At that same moment, an old lady, who was raking and collecting hay and making the noise, saw me and screamed with fright. It took me a moment to realise that I was the cause of the blood-curdling wail, as the old woman, discarding her rake, threw both arms in the air and ran.

"A ghost! It's a ghost! I've seen a ghost!" she was shouting hysterically although there was no one around to hear her except me. After she had run about a hundred yards away, she stopped and turned around to see what was really inside the haystack. I crawled out, bits of grass and hay stuck all over me, and called out to her not to be frightened. But the old woman, keeping her distance, refused to come anywhere near me.

As I continued to cover great distances over the endless plains, my food ran out and once again I became a scavenger, living off the land, or begging help from brief encounters with local people. Often, I only saw people from a distance. Sometimes it was a few herdsmen or a shepherd, at other times it was farm workers. I even saw a camel train where the camels were pulling two-wheeled carts. After many days or weeks, I found myself walking through a large area of the country growing only watermelons. Row upon row of these enormous fruits grew close to the ground, seemingly lying there just for the taking. As there was no other food available, I picked a large melon. By this time, I had acquired a proper knife from one of my kindly hosts and had long since abandoned the home-made tool from the prison camp. I sat down and carefully sliced the melon into about six segments and thoroughly enjoyed biting into the juicy fruit, spitting out all the annoying little black pips. As I sat there enjoying the refreshing change of diet, something small and intensely yellow fluttered by. It was a small butterfly and I watched as it landed and seemed to disappear. The underside of its wings was the same colour as the leaves, so it was perfectly camouflaged. Once I knew they were there, I began to spot many of these bright butterflies in flight.

I continued for many miles, stopping periodically to slice open and eat a melon. At first, the new diet was a welcome change, but with only melons for food, it was not long before I began to have a problem with my digestion. To begin with I had the kind of stomach cramps I had become familiar with on this epic journey, but this rapidly developed into something much worse. For the first time I was glad that I was travelling alone since I had to resort to walking without my trousers on. This was the only way to preserve my clean clothing since I had to relieve myself so frequently. Mortifying as this would have been had I encountered another person; I was nevertheless thankful that I had been provided with some freely available nourishment. I was never more thankful than when I reached a river and was able to restore the condition of my personal hygiene. Food had inevitably once again become my highest priority and I had no choice about what to eat – I just had to eat what was available at the time. Any farm produce along the road automatically belonged to me, and I always said a grateful prayer to the people who had planted it.

CHAPTER 21

THE CASPIAN SEA (AUTUMN 1941)

The first clue I had that I was approaching the coast of the Caspian Sea was when I sighted a few distant seagulls. But there were still hundreds of miles to cover. I had to cross large areas of marsh; thinking back I guess I must have been somewhere near the Aral Sea which at that time was a vast lake. At times the country became heavily populated, and I was extra cautious in my movements, hoping to avoid the notice of any NKVD or military personnel. Although by this time the Soviet leadership had agreed to let the Polish people go free in what they called an Amnesty, I had no idea about this, and I doubt that any of the people I encountered would have had any knowledge of this or of any other international dealings.

By this time the country seemed to be fully mobilised. I saw tremendous movements of military vehicles, columns of trucks, and trains carrying hundreds of tanks. Seeing this cheered me up as I hoped that western Poland at least would be liberated from the German army. But I also saw that a great deal of military hardware and personnel were being transported south which I found somewhat mystifying. At the time I had no idea that the Soviets had invaded Persia in collaboration with the British army. I was only aware that army transports and troops were criss-crossing the country's rail and road networks and that even more food and raw materials were being requisitioned. Food was becoming increasingly scarce as was the generosity of the people.

Fortunately, ordinary citizens ignored me; they had their own concerns. Once again, I was looking like a scarecrow, with my skeletal-like appearance, and my unwashed clothing had become shabby and ragged through sleeping outside. I was not at all worried about how I looked; I only worried about food. Knowing that I must by now be approaching the end of my journey, my thoughts turned to home, to Rovno.

"What shall I do if I ever get back home?" I asked myself aloud. When no other people were within ear shot, I often found myself thinking aloud. "I will organise a gang of people to carry out sabotage on a large scale," I answered myself. "And," I said loudly and with conviction, "I want everyone in the world to know that Siberia consists mainly of concentration camps, not just holding thousands of us Polish people, but also thousands of Russians!" I wanted to be able to tell the world about the Orthodox priests and so many others who were being punished for criticising the system, and also about the treatment of the remnants of former wealthy people whose lands had been confiscated. "But first I have to survive and reach my goal. Never say die," I told myself.

The screeching cries of hundreds of seagulls heralded my eventual arrival at the coast of the Caspian Sea. The first settlement that I came across was a small fishing village. I continued walking right up to the water's edge and just stared out at the sea, hardly trusting my eyes, telling myself that this was no hallucination but that I really had made it all the way. An elderly gentleman, who was sitting outside a small cottage mending some nets, looked curiously at me. Thinking that he might be willing to offer me some food, I approached him hopefully.

"I have travelled a great distance and am very hungry. Do you have any spare food?" I asked him, "I have no roubles, but I am willing to work for my food," I offered. He nodded and gestured to me to sit down on the bench next to him.

"I have fish," he said simply, putting his work to one side and going into his cottage. He returned shortly with some salted fish and a small hunk of black bread on a wooden board and handed these to me. "When you have eaten you can tell me where you have journeyed from," he said kindly. His accent made me think he came from somewhere south of the Caucasus, maybe Georgia. Having washed down the fish, which I had made myself eat slowly, with a cup of cool water, I told him that I had escaped from a prison camp in Siberia.

"We are not criminals," I said, "we are just ordinary Polish people, but the Soviet government needed labourers to cut down forests and build roads, so they deported us to Siberia," I explained. The old man nodded.

"We have heard about these camps. For many years, even before the Revolution, people were sent there as punishment. Some even chose to go there when there was famine in their own land," he told me, "Many people have tried to escape to the west or south into Persia, but I think they have mostly come from somewhere north of Moscow, I don't remember anyone coming from eastern Siberia before."

"Yes, that's where I would like to go, to Persia," I said, glad that he accepted my story without the usual interrogation that I had become so used to when meeting new people.

"It would not be easy to walk around the sea," he warned. "There are many soldiers and much fighting on the border with Persia and in the mountain passes. The Persians may mistake you for a Russian spy and the Russians may take you for a Persian spy!" he said laughing slightly at his dark humour.

"What do you suggest?" I asked, hoping that his local knowledge would prove to be valuable.

"The best way to get there is on a small fishing boat that no one will be interested in; but you would have to pay for the journey," he said, nodding his old head as if agreeing with himself. All the while there was a twinkle in his eyes as he looked at me and a kindly smile hovered about his mouth. I felt very safe with this man who I realised reminded me somehow of my own grandfather.

"I have already told you that I have no roubles," I said, "Do you know anyone who is looking to hire a worker so that I can earn my passage?" I asked.

"Don't worry," he said, with the obligatory nod, "you can stay with me and share my fish while we see what can be done." I gladly accepted his offer.

During the day I worked in his garden removing weeds, feeding his chickens, and doing any other odd jobs that needed attention. In the evenings we talked about politics and religion; he wasn't at all shy of either of these subjects and had some very strong opinions that he was willing to share, uncowed by the repressive regime that we all lived under.

"This government that we have in Russia now is terrible," he told me, "It is terrible for the Russian people, and those who are responsible will be punished one day for their crimes against humanity. We must pray, and wait for better times," he added crossing himself as he spoke. There were a few Orthodox icons in his house, and he was evidently a religious man struggling in the new secular world around him.

With the old gentleman's help, I tried to find a way round the problem of purchasing safe, and discreet, passage across the sea. He did suggest that one solution would be for me to stay with him permanently.

"You are very kind, and I am happy here," I told him, "But I have travelled so far and do not want to give up at this stage, when I am so close to my goal." He seemed to accept this and offered to take me to some friends who he thought would be able to help.

"I have some friends in another village; they have a bigger boat than mine, with many deck hands, and can go further across the sea. Perhaps they will take you out fishing with them and drop you off somewhere along the Persian coast," he said hopefully.

We made the trip to the other village and spoke with the friends. But we found no one willing to take such a risk. They believed that if they were caught, they would be severely punished and might even be sent to Siberia themselves for committing a crime against the State. However, they did suggest that I move to another small port a little further along the coast where boats regularly took passengers to Persia. This seemed a good suggestion and I said my thanks and goodbyes to the elderly gentleman, with optimism, but still lacking any roubles to pay my way.

On arriving at the small port in the evening, I found an empty boat, and decided to climb aboard while I had the chance to do so unobserved. There was a large pile of nets lying on the deck, so I decided to hide under them, pulling the heavy mesh over me, and went to sleep. I stayed on the boat for several days, sleeping under the nets at night, waiting for something to happen but no one came. Reluctantly, and very hungry, I decided to try elsewhere.

Instead of just leaping on the nearest empty boat, I realised I needed to reconnoitre the harbour and make some serious plans. During the daytime I studied the movements of the various boats but returned to my hiding place under the fishing nets to sleep at night. There didn't seem to be much possibility of stowing away on the small boats since they didn't appear to travel very far, and certainly couldn't have been going to Persia. I decided I needed yet again to ask for help. Experience had taught me that young people were never helpful, so I approached an old gentleman who I had noticed hanging around the port and told him of my predicament. He was clearly suspicious of me – by then I was in a bedraggled and starving state again.

"Who you are? What are you doing here? Why are you trying to get out of Russia?" he questioned in the manner of the kind of interrogation I had by now become so accustomed to. His own suspicious nature made me feel reluctant to be honest with him; I was fearful that if I told him the whole truth that he would hand me over to the authorities.

"I am a Muslim," I said, "that is why I am trying to get to Persia."

"I don't believe you," he said, "I think you have come over the border from Persia to spy on our military positions; perhaps you are a saboteur." He was clearly unconvinced by my story and by not telling the truth I seemed to have put myself in a very dangerous situation. I couldn't change my story now, so instead I elaborated, hoping to convince him.

"I have come from the Tartar settlement in Poland. We are only a very small minority group of people and we have remained in Poland to this day; we have our own mosques there," I told him earnestly, hoping that he would accept my story. He remained unconvinced but decided to help me anyway.

"I can give you some advice," he said reluctantly, "on condition that you do not disclose to anyone that you received any information from me about how to get into Persia." I willingly agreed to this; I knew it would be regarded as treason on his part if he was found to have helped me escape from Russia.

"You need to go further along the coast to the next fishing village that also has a port for transporting goods and passengers. They have larger boats there and they travel regularly to Persia," he told me, although he still didn't give me any advice about how to obtain passage. However, I followed his advice and continued further along the coast until I came to a larger settlement with a proper port designed for much larger boats for shipping goods and people. I still didn't know how I was to get on board with no money, no ticket, and no papers. I sat down and watched all the comings and goings for several hours. When boats were being made ready, there was always someone standing at the bottom of the gangway checking passengers on.

I found myself watching one porter in particular because he had a strange gait that was always made worse when he was carrying his heavy load aboard, but when he returned it was hardly noticeable. I wondered idly if he had been injured, or born with some kind of deformity, and suddenly realised that while I had been following his movements, he hadn't been stopped for checks even though he made several journeys on and off the boat.

"That's it!" I told myself, "I just need to pretend to be a porter and help with the loading." I strolled nonchalantly up to the group of porters and seeing a large box that had so far been avoided, heaved it onto my chest so that it obscured my face, and staggered up the gangway while the man who was checking the passengers helpfully moved out of my way. Having disposed of my load I looked around for a suitable hiding place.

The boat looked like a rusty old barge with some containers dumped on the top for the crew. There were a number of other passengers already milling round so I decided to just stand around with them and follow their lead as to which part of the boat they would occupy during the voyage. I reasoned that if I just stayed out of people's way and didn't talk to them, they wouldn't take any notice of me. I found a suitably out-of-the-way place, sat down, and waited for the boat to set sail.

The engines started up, and belching thick smoke, we slowly chugged out of the port. After a few hours out on the open sea I began to think about food and drink and saw with envy that several of my fellow passengers had brought provisions with them. But I didn't dare draw attention to myself by begging for any kind of sustenance - I knew I would just have to wait until I was safely out of reach of the NKVD.

As night fell and darkness swallowed us up, a strong wind began to blow. The boat began to pitch and roll, the rusty hull creaking and groaning. As the nausea rose in me, I began to retch painfully, but there was nothing inside me to bring up but bile. The other passengers seemed unconcerned, most of them able to sleep through the night, evidently suitably hardened to the journey. The sea was still choppy the following morning and as the hours passed, I became more comfortable with the swell and dip of the waves. By late afternoon we were in sight of what I hoped was the coast of Persia, but we then continued many more hours following the line of the coast until we finally turned into a small fishing harbour.

I had no real idea where we had landed, or who the authorities would be, Persian, Russian, or British, and of course I was still without papers or any form of identification. I left the boat the same way I had boarded it, by joining the gang who were unloading the cargo. My disembarking went unnoticed. But looking around me I realised that I would have to go through a control point to be able to leave the area where goods were unloaded. Dehydrated, starving, and with no strength left in me, I had no option but to walk through the only exit available and hope that I was no longer on Russian territory. The guard on duty, to my horror speaking in Russian, demanded to see my papers, and then proceeded to put me under arrest. I was taken to a building where the guard left me while he found out what was to be done with me.

"Where am I?" I wanted to know, "Am I in Persia?"

"Yes, but it is under Russian and British occupation. You are not allowed to travel without papers."

In my state of complete exhaustion, I couldn't understand what he was saying. How could Persia be under British and Russian occupation? But I perfectly understood when the guard's superior officer told him that I should be put back on the boat and sent back where I had come from. At his point, the sheer terror of being sent back to Russia sent me into a frenzy. I screamed and shouted in my desperation.

"I am not Russian! I don't want to go back there! You can't send me back! I won't go!"

More officials arrived, I was so distressed that I could hardly make myself understood and was thrown into even more confusion by the sight of Persians, Russians, and what seemed to be soldiers from India in British uniforms. I was interrogated at length in Russian; they wanted to know who I was, where I had come from, and where I wanted to go. All the time I insisted that I was Polish and wanted to find the remnants of the Polish army and join them in fighting for our freedom.

Eventually they took me to an office block and, still unsure what to do with me, locked me in one of the offices. Was I to be held captive yet again just when I thought I had finally escaped from it all? They seemed to forget about me; I was still locked in as night fell and no one had been to see me. I went to sleep on the floor, grateful to be left in peace.

By the next morning I was desperate to relieve myself, so I started banging on the door and walls of the office hoping someone would hear me. Finally, a man came and opened the door and was clearly astonished at my appearance.

"I have been locked in all night and I need to use the toilet facilities," I managed to tell him. I can only imagine what I must have looked like by now, a dried-up skeleton of a human with filthy matted hair. The man took me to where I needed to go, and then, after considering what he should do with me, arranged for me to be admitted to the local hospital.

At last, I was to be taken care of and permitted to feel safe. My tattered and filthy clothes were taken away and I was given pyjamas to wear. Someone washed and fed me. I only had one thought, "Never say die," and I hadn't.

After about two weeks in the hospital a group of people arrived looking very much as I must have done when I had arrived there. I lay there listening in to their conversation, and gradually it dawned on me that I wasn't listening to Russian but Polish! They were from Poland! It transpired that they, like me, had come from Soviet Russia; they were also former prisoners wanting to join a Polish army to fight against the Germans.

All in all, my escape had taken approximately ten months or more, and although there was no way of recording the mileage of my journey, I must have covered at least four thousand miles.

HISTORICAL NOTE:

It has only been possible to estimate the timing of Viktor's journey but knowing that he ate melons as he approached the region of the Caspian Sea puts the time of year as late summer or early autumn.

The British invaded Persia (Iran) from the west in August 1941, codenamed Operation Countenance, and at the same time, the Soviets invaded from Turkmenistan in the north of Persia. The British division that proceeded as far as the shores of the Caspian Sea included brigades from the 10th Indian Infantry Division, commanded by Major-General Slim, who is reputed to have said, the troops "drank beer on the shores of the Caspian." One of the Soviet objectives was to capture the Caspian Sea port of Bandar Pahlavi. By March of 1942 the 10th Indian Infantry had already left the region.

The so-called Amnesty of the Poles in the USSR was agreed in July, and the decree issued on August 12th, 1941. However, it was often many months before people in the most remote camps were made aware of it. When the Poles were released, many were simply told they were now free and were left to their own devices and made their own way out of the country. For others, transport was arranged, and hundreds of thousands were transported south to various assembly points in Kazakhstan and Uzbekistan. Many were already so weakened by their stay in Siberia that they did not survive this journey. Many thousands more died in the typhus-ridden relocation camps. The first official evacuations were in March 1942.

Some of those who survived the train journey to the port of Krasnovodsk on the Caspian Sea, didn't survive long enough to board the ships. The Soviet ships that were provided were overcrowded and ill equipped and many perished on the sea crossing. Some who reached the Persian port of Pahlevi and freedom did not survive to see it.

A copy of the next part of Mary's typed manuscript is given below:

<u>Pre-war Poland</u>

I remember my grandfather very well for his great kindness. In their home they had a large oil painting of him, uniformed with a long spike on top of his helmet, holding his sword and sitting on horseback. However, this painting had to be relegated to the attic because anyone who had willingly served in the Austrian army was not regarded with favour. He was very kind but ruled the household with strict military precision. Grandmother had to report to him every week on the household supplies and account for every zloty she had spent.

He rarely visited us in Rovno and when he did, he stayed only for a few hours. He was a countryman at heart and only lived for his fruit trees. Mother, my sister and I visited him frequently, usually when father was away at work, and I loved the time I spent with him in the orchards. He was a deeply religious person; he did not drink socially, but following his old army custom, every morning before breakfast, he had one tot of pure spirits or vodka — which he firmly believed kept him healthy. This must have been the reason for his good health because he had not visited a doctor since having his original medical examination on joining the army. He died when he was over 100 years of age, just before the war started in 1939. He was found lying on the ground under one of his beloved fruit trees. The family thought he was asleep, but on being unable to wake him, discovered he had died, in May 1939.

In his will, grandfather left me his officer's silver sword. I was very proud of this, and shortly after having it I cut my toes very badly (having the scar to this day) whilst practising fencing. The sword was later buried with the rest of mother's treasures. Grandfather had left me also a very expensive revolver which was to be given to me when I was older, but unfortunately the war overtook events and I never received this. I was also heir to the house and orchards on the death of grandmother.

As children we rarely saw father as he worked away from home six days a week and we were only together on Sundays. He was involved in secret government work and as we lived close to the Russian border, he needed protection from their secret agents and had a bodyguard on a permanent basis. In addition, we at home had a specially trained Alsatian guard dog to watch out for intruders.

My sister and I had a very happy childhood and from the age of four were taught to ski, skate, and ride as well as other sports, although my preference was always for riding a bicycle rather than a horse. Our education included political indoctrination from the lowest age, love of our country, religion, as well as all the usual subjects. From the age of 8 — 11 I was sent away to a boarding school for the sons of officers and ex-officers, with the intention of preparing me for a military career. At age 12 I returned home and attended a private College in Rovno. Whilst at this college I learned to shoot and had further general preparation for life in the services. I also joined the Air Force cadets and by the age of 12 I had made several jumps from a training tower for parachute training. We spent a great deal of time orienteering and living off the land and had to spend many nights finding our way through the forest with only a compass, torch and maps (this training was to save my life later on).

As we lived so close to the Russian border, our college students were given the task of tracking down and watching for Russian intruders who came over the border in hordes. Despite a strong border guard, intruders and saboteurs entered Poland to try to destabilise the country. Our own police and border guards (called KOP) were unable to arrest everyone who came over and our college boys were used as a third line of defence in reporting suspicious-looking people to the authorities. The intruders generally lived rough in our forests and made for small villages where they had contacts and were then able to send reports back to Russia about our newly built military installations, river bridges and railway lines etc.

At the same time as tracking down spies from Russia, we would also come across intelligence officers from Germany who were infiltrating the German colony living around the Volyn area. They started supplying guns, ammunition, and propaganda leaflets mainly against the Jews who were leaving Germany and Russia by the thousands. On one occasion about six of us college boys saw in the forest a very suspicious-looking man hiding in the bushes. From the distance we watched his every movement without him knowing we were there. We spent several

171

hours watching him and then decided to report him to the authorities. One of us ran to the police to report his presence, whilst five of us watched him from a distance — our aim being not to lose sight of him. Unfortunately, one of our lads got too close and the German caught hold of him and asked, "Why are you here and what are you doing?" When our friend said he was just going for a walk in the forest, the German took out a knife and was just about to cut his throat. On seeing this, the rest of us rushed out with our Scout's knives at the ready and attacked him. While he was preoccupied with the first boy, he had failed to notice the approach of the rest of us. We disarmed him and pinned him to the ground until the police arrived and arrested him. This man spoke perfect Polish and Russian as well as his mother tongue and he turned out to be a secret agent. After about two days searching the forest, all his belongings were discovered — all sorts of sabotage equipment, changes of clothing for disguise purposes, bedding, and iron rations. The authorities did not disclose to us boys the whole story, but we received grateful acknowledgement together with a radio for the school in appreciation of our patriotic work.

There were many such instances of this nature, you may say it happened every week in one or other part of the town and forest. As well as our college boys, the Boy Scouts were involved, and other civilian organisations watched daily for such people. The forests around our area were quite dangerous because people came over the border from Russia for illegal purposes.

As well as criminals and spies, everyday crowds of ordinary Russians escaped to Poland from the communist regime, and others came over because they were desperately short of food. They had great difficulty in crossing the border because the *guards were instructed to shoot to kill any of their citizens who were escaping into Poland and thus informing the world of their terrible living conditions. The League of Nations knew of the situation but did very little to help these refugees and when the Polish government complained to the League of Nations, Russia always denied the situation and said it was Polish propaganda against the Communist regime.*

Towards the end of 1938, Germany increased the number of spies and 5th columnists sent into Poland, and they also started to train the Ukrainian minority groups living in Poland into SS units, to be prepared to help with the 1939 invasion. Around our town we had a large colony of Czech and Germans, who had been sent many years ago by the Tsar (Catherine the Great) of Russia to cultivate this part of the country when it belonged to Russia. These people were given the best agricultural land and were very prosperous. For this reason, they were supporting Russia and they often helped the foreign spies.

On the day Germany invaded Poland, the Ukrainian SS units created havoc by going into action, destroying bridges, railway lines and military installations. In appreciation for this help, Germany had promised these people that the Ukraine would be given to them when Germany had taken the whole of Poland.

Just before the war started, we heard that England, France, and America were going to support us with our problem with Germany. We were all prepared to fight, but Britain forbade us to mobilise our forces, saying that this would inflame the Germans into taking action, because they would then say that Poland had started the war by mobilising. This was a great dis-service to us, as if our army had been ready, we could have held Germany for a longer period and may even have won the war if Russia had not invaded from the Eastern front. Our enemies have never attacked us singly but always in twos or threes. Every one man, including students and boy scouts were ready and glad to give their lives for their country. My mother told me "Remember it is your duty to fight and give your life, if necessary, for your country because you have never lost your freedom and you do not know what it means to be occupied by a foreign force".

We lived in a beautiful small town and there was always something interesting to see and do. Close by there was a cavalry garrison, a military aerodrome, and other military personnel. We had a mixture of religions, Catholic, Orthodox, Jews and a few Protestants – all living together in harmony; it was forbidden to denigrate any other religion or nationality – all were Polish citizens regardless of creed. Every Sunday the cavalry military orchestra marched through the town into our church and took part in the Mass. We had a choir of 500 which, together with the military orchestra, gave a wonderful performance of hymns, and the roof and the windows of the church often rattled with the volume of music.

Every Autumn the army would return to barracks after three months manoeuvres and over 10,000 men, horses, and tanks – as well as heavy artillery – marched through the town for many hours. The majority of the townsfolk were out to meet them with flowers and sweets, to welcome them back, and all the families on the route of the march would decorate their houses with flags and flowers. The townspeople were very friendly with the army personnel and always treated them with great respect. In return, every Christmas and Easter, the army entertained the townspeople to parties, and every weekend their orchestras played in the local parks and arranged military displays and fireworks. Besides this, the army provided help for the orphanage, and every day local schoolchildren could go along to the barracks after school to eat the food which was left over from the army kitchen. Any family who needed help was always able to see the military commandant who would give assistance with food or clothing.

Another favourite attraction in the summer was a large trade fair held in the park. Exhibitors came from all over Poland, with engineering products, fabrics, chemicals, building materials and many novelties that were being produced at that time. The town kids spent many happy hours collecting samples, literature and watching demonstrations. At the same time there was a large circus with the trade fair and that was always a great excitement for us. A different orchestra played in the park every day and during the evenings the young people were able to dance until midnight. All the shops around the exhibition stayed open for 24 hours and in the centre of the town the restaurants remained open all night to cater for the many visitors from Hungary, Romania, Czechoslovakia and our other neighbours, with the exception of Russia – as they were not allowed to leave their country during the Stalin days.

In the warm summer evenings, we also had gypsy bands to entertain us with their dancing and singing. They would build fires in the clearings in the woods and invite the townsfolk out for an evening of musical entertainment – afterwards making a collection.

The river Horyn was nearby where we spent a lot of our summer days swimming, sailing and fishing. The fish were very plentiful and varied, and this was a popular pastime for young and old alike. The river was in beautiful surroundings, overgrown with willow trees and with masses of different birds. The soil around us was very rich, and our markets were bursting with fruit and vegetables – I remember once fetching a bucket of cherries for preserving for about 4p – it was hardly worth the farmers picking them. We had such warm summers that tomatoes grew outside, and no one ever needed a greenhouse. We picked mushrooms from the forest and dried them for winter soups etc. We also picked wild strawberries and bilberries. If you were poor, there was plenty of food available just for the picking. Locally, hops were grown, sweetcorn, wheat, and rye – we had some of the richest soil in the whole of Europe. Our summers were tropical, but the winters were arctic. Poland was quite rapidly developing, and the majority of people enjoyed quite a comfortable standard of living. The prices in the shops were stable for many years.

We had a very full social life, mother had lots of friends round to visit us in the week whilst father was away at the office. During the hot weather we had barbeques and garden parties for our family and school friends. Our garden was most productive, with fruit, vegetables, tomatoes, and salads etc. We had one enormous pear tree with so much fruit that even we, our family, and friends, could not eat it all, so mother sold the entire crop to Jewish merchants who picked and packed them and sold them in their stores.

Sunday for us was always a wonderful day, as it was the only day father spent with us at home. We were all on our best behaviour – we tried to please him and make it a happy family day, and yet at the same time both of us children were slightly afraid because his standards were so high. We actually had two ways of life at home. Monday to Saturday with mother was relaxed and casual, and Saturday evening when father arrived home until early Monday morning when he left for the office were always very formal with good behaviour expected. When he arrived on Saturday evening, he always brought us kids a large bag of sweets and chocolates, and also a present for mother. This was to say sorry for not being with us during the week. On Sunday morning we were questioned closely on our progress at school and what we had been doing with ourselves during the week. He always looked through our homework books and asked us to read for him from our schoolbooks. After either his approval or disapproval of our work, he told us what he expected from us the following week. Many Sundays he did not have time to go to church, so we had our own family prayers in the house. We had a small altar with a crucifix and our own prayer books. Father would read, say a prayer and then we sang a hymn, which I never enjoyed as I preferred Mass in church.

Afterwards, we had a programme arranged for the rest of the day. If the weather was fine, we sometimes went to a restaurant for lunch and then a walk in the park in the afternoon, or a walk in the forest. Other times we went boating on the local river and sometimes we all went for a ride in the forest. The stables would deliver four horses to the house at about 2pm and we would spend the afternoon riding. After our ride we either took the horses back to the stables or they collected them from home. I myself would have preferred to ride my bike, but we had to do what father wanted and that was that. In winter we regularly went skiing which I learned from the age of four and over the years had become quite proficient. All our family enjoyed outdoor activities.

We had family get-togethers with singing and dancing (which my father adored) or his friends brought their musical instruments round, and we had a musical evening, with father playing the violin and mother playing the piano. For the odd occasions we were on our own, we used to get father to tell us fairy stories, for which he had a real gift, and we were just happy to sit with him. I always followed him around like a little dog and could not bear to part with him on Monday mornings.

As we approached 1939, we were very concerned that, after just over 20 years of freedom and independence, we would again be in trouble, and we all started to hope for a miracle to happen to save us. We knew the war was close, as father and many others were recalled to the army in August 1939. This was done as discreetly as possible so that our enemies were unaware of our actions. When he left, father told me that I was "the man of the house" and to look after my mother and sister. My responsibility was to defend them and find food for them if it got short. He gave me his revolver and, as he had to leave hurriedly, he asked me to bury all the family silver and other valuables in the garden.

Just before war commenced, a lot of father's friends gathered in our home to discuss the possibility of war. They feared this was approaching, as the Germans were arming themselves and looking for expansion in the east. As Poland had only limited funds to spend on armaments, and also had not been able to build up sufficient industry to produce arms, the authorities were looking for any way to avoid trouble with Germany, but this proved impossible. In the meantime, Russia promised Poland they would not attack them, but we did not believe this promise, as we were a capitalist country, and they were red hot communists. They detested us to the extent that on the border the Russian people were not even allowed to look across into Poland. The terrible conditions in which the vast majority of

Russians lived at that time were concealed by their government and no Polish persons were allowed to enter Russia for any reason.

I went for my summer holiday in August 1939 with the Boy Scouts and during this holiday we spent a lot of time preparing for the war. Every day we had political discussions, training in sabotage, use of different weapons and explosives, throwing dummy grenades, and learning to recognise the uniforms and ranks of different sections of the German army. We were all trained to use various types of equipment in case we were needed to help with an underground army. We were very keen and many of us actually looked forward to any forthcoming trouble – as boys do.

Additional comments from the interview with Viktor:

"I had a good education, because my father saw that his son was educated, so at the age of four I was in school – I was the only son.

We had a nanny for us children. But we didn't have a car. Only very rich people had a car, but we had a chauffeur who came to collect us. People used to say you are very rich because you have a car, but the car wasn't ours – it was a government car. We had everything we wanted. But we had something on which I wasn't keen – discipline. Father was very strict on discipline – politeness all the time. The other kids were free, but I had to do exactly what I was told. Eventually you get used to it. Afterward – when you are older – you appreciate it. I had to kiss mother's hands – etiquette. When guests came you had to know your place.

My education was terrific. Why? Because my father had big power. I went to a special boarding school. It was a military school for the sons of officers, paid for by the government. The discipline was too much. We had to learn languages. In scouts I learned parachute jumping from a tower – father saw that I did everything possible, including shooting. Parents give us pocket money – me and my sister – father gave us pocket money. It was never enough for me – whatever they gave me I could do with more, because I had so many hobbies. Mother would go to the shops and bring me so and so. When the war began my mother told me to bury all our family treasure, my inheritance, in a deep hole in Grandfather's orchard, under a pear tree. I hope it is still there."

"I remember playing with Marshal Pilsudski's daughters."

Invasion of Poland

Immediately on returning home for the beginning of college term on the 1ˢᵗ of September, the war started during the night, when German bombers attacked our local railway station and the surrounding town, destroying lot of army equipment. Looking back, it was difficult to believe that I was looking forward to fighting – not then knowing the horrors of war. College was immediately suspended, and all able-bodied civilians were directed to help with the preparations to defend the town. General mobilisation had still not taken place so as not to give the Germans an excuse for attacking us. During the day we dug trenches to protect ourselves against further air attacks and I saw men actually crying with frustration that they could not enlist. The civil authorities organised help for the hospitals and families of those who would be joining the army. Food was stored in places protected from destruction and large amounts of money were collected from the public for the war effort. Many men had volunteered for suicide missions — to strap explosives around their bodied and destroy enemy tanks. In the meantime, our Rovno Garrison moved towards the west to defend Warsaw, not knowing that Russia would be attacking us from the east.

Very early in the morning of 17th of September, hundreds of Russian planes bombed roads, railway lines and river bridges, to be followed by endless columns of tanks crossing the Polish border, with hordes of troops, cavalry and artillery advancing towards us — without any declaration of war. Unfortunately, our local garrison had moved to the west to fight the German advance, so we had no defence at all. When crossing the border, the Russian Army told us they were here to help fight the Germans so we should not oppose them because they were our friends; eventually we found this was not true and they were attacking Poland to take half of the country — as agreed between Ribbentrop and Molotov in early 1939. We were still waiting for any help from the west, but this did not come.

We started to organise ourselves to resist the Russians, knowing that it would mean fighting on two fronts. Nevertheless, we caused them great difficulties with our underground army. It was difficult to fight Russia, as the border stretched from Lithuania to Romania and was an enormous length, and to be able to defend such a long border an entire army was needed, but this was fighting the Germans. We knew our cavalry was very little defence against their tanks, but our officers did their very best and were world famous for their bravery. The Russians had detested us ever since we defeated them in the 1920s and almost succeeded in destroying communisms, and this was purely

181

a revenge attack. When the Russian army controlled half of Poland, we were very surprised what a poorly equipped and badly maintained army it was. It was only the sheer numbers which over-ran us.

From then, we boy scouts started our sabotage. We were to create as much havoc as possible. We were organised into groups of five scouts, ages ranging from twelve to seventeen, with co-operation between all units but only knowing each other's number and assumed names. My number was 555 and I was known as Teddy. We also included girls in the groups; they were absolutely invaluable and extremely brave. During my time with these groups, we blew up a railway line, robbed food trains and distributed food to elderly civilians in the town, we stole rifles from Russian soldiers by various tricks – the young Russians were so green and nervous that it was quite easy to hoodwink them. Eventually, with the help of stolen uniforms, we were able to get practically anywhere amongst them and stole grenades and other equipment. We were not always successful and some of our scouts were executed on the spot when found out. The invading army had no mercy at all with anyone found in the wrong place at the wrong time. Our favourite form of attack was to throw a grenade into one of their tanks. On one occasion we managed to entice two Russian officers to a party with girls and vodka. When they were drunk, we overpowered them, stripped them of their uniform and weapons and passed these on to our underground army. This was only in the early days of the occupation, as later on it was realised that the population was not co-operating with them, and they had to be more alert. By then, their soldiers could not safely walk in the town on their own, but only in groups of three and four.

As the Russian troops consolidated their position, they started systematically to strip the shops, factories, and private houses. Whatever it was possible to move they loaded into trains and took into Russia. From our house they took blankets, clothes, cooking utensils, small pieces of furniture and our grand piano. The ordinary soldiers could not believe we lived in such comfort. The troops had very little to eat and were taking food from the townspeople and local villages. During the hours of darkness, they attacked farms, taking away anything edible, either dead or alive. Their staple food was porridge made from rye, and black bread. Their army food was inadequate, evidently mighty Russia could not feed their own army, and afterwards, although they were our enemies, we felt sorry for them. Additionally, their uniforms were in rags and tatters. Many soldiers carried their rifles on a piece of string instead of a leather strap. Their shoes were never cleaned, but they only covered them with a sort of smelly liquid to preserve them from wet weather. We could not bear to stand anywhere near them, as the hygiene of the ordinary troops was totally inadequate. We started to make jokes about the mighty Russian army and even the soldiers themselves said, "We have very good technology but no culture at all yet."

In early October, I decided to go into Russia to visit Father's cousin, as I had never seen him but knew he lived in a town called Zaslaw – about thirty miles from Poland. I wanted to let them know where we lived in case he ever came into Poland. We had been unable to contact them for many years – the last contact being made in 1922, but I knew his name and approximately where he lived, although I had not got the exact address. It took me five days to get there because, although Poland was now occupied by the Red Army, they still guarded the border with special troops and dogs. The land

183

around the border was ploughed and raked every day so that the guards could detect any footprints, and in many places the fences were protected by electric wires — this was to keep their own people inside Russia. I knew of all these difficulties but decided to risk it and go.

My biggest problem was actually crossing the border, and I spent one whole day hiding in the bushes watching the guards. I wanted to plot my route so that I could scramble from bush to bush without leaving footprints. At one stage one of the guards was only five yards from me and my heart sank with fright; luckily for me the soldier moved on and I jumped to another bush which he had previously searched around. Eventually I got across the border and then walked only during the night into Zaslaw. On arriving in the town, I had to start looking for my family, and more problems arose. The town was full of troops and KGB — always on the lookout for suspicious-looking people, checking the internal passports of anyone they were not happy with; in those days it was necessary to have an internal passport to travel from one town to another.

I managed to make my way into the park and asked a kindly-looking man if he by any chance knew my family or where the area of the town was that I thought they lived in. He had never heard of them but gave me the name and address of a Jewish family who lived in the area I was looking for. As soon as it was dark, I made my way to this Jewish house. They recognised that I spoke with a Polish accent and decided to help me. I was extremely grateful to them, but they forbad me to go out in daylight in case anyone recognised my clothing which was not typically Russian and report me to the authorities. Every fifth person in Russia was an informer — in fact, even the schoolchildren watched their own parents. The Jewish family

*had not heard of my father's cousin, they sent me on further
to a friend of theirs in another district who they thought could
help me. The other family lived in Lenin Street, and they also
questioned me carefully to find out whether I was genuinely
Polish and looking for my family. When they were quite sure
they made investigations on my behalf and found out that,
although my family had previously lived in their area, they
had since moved. Fortunately for me they found where they
were living and, under cover of darkness I made my way to
their house.*

During the interview, Viktor told me that a lady found
him sleeping in a doorway and she helped him find his
father's cousin. Sometime later he heard that this lady
had been murdered by the NKVD for feeding Germans.

*Finally, I found the house and my family; imagine the joy
and tears on both sides when we met. My father's cousin
Joseph was an army officer, in charge of supplying all the
building materials needed for the construction of a large army
installation. Compared to the average households, he lived in
luxury only found in the elite Party homes. They had a lovely
villa, just outside the town, with a cook and a chauffeur at
his disposal; he had access to the special shops for Party
members and could obtain anything he wished. His wife, Stella,
a most beautiful woman of about forty years of age, possessed
ten mink coats (much to my great surprise) and their main
pleasure was in buying clothes and socialising. Every wardrobe
in the house was full (on returning home my mother could
hardly believe this).*

*Joseph was an extremely clever and popular person. He had
originally come from a wealthy land-owning family but had*

managed to conceal this in order to make a career for himself in the army. Practically every night they entertained or went visiting, mostly with other army officers and their wives. Their parties generally consisted of heavy drinking, unlimited food, and music and dancing. They introduced me to their friends as "Vitaly (Russian for Viktor) from the West" [Vitaly means 'full of life' and is not in fact a Russian version of Viktor] and as he was with trusted friends no further questions were asked. I was amazed to see in their home some of the things looted from Poland, and their especial treasure was a Polish gramophone and records. They had various small pieces of furniture and Stella had lots of dress material, mostly pure silk and other expensive fabrics manufactured in Lodz (a Polish city specializing in manufacturing all types of materials). Joseph had at least fifteen superior quality Polish suits. They also had curtains and carpets from Poland. The goods stolen from our shops and homes had very quickly been distributed to the high-ranking officers and Party officials. Other items included a bicycle and a Polish radio. At that time, it was an offence to have a radio, in case 'propaganda' was picked up from abroad. Most Russian families had cable radio with only Russian programmes.

Before the first world war about fifteen thousand Polish families lived in this part of the Ukraine; there had been five Polish catholic churches and a Franciscan Monastery. After the Revolution they were all closed and used mostly as warehouses. The Orthodox church had been demolished and the building material used to build a school. Joseph and Stella took me to meet another family in the town; they kissed and hugged me and many of them cried, because they had not met anyone from Poland for many years. They were not allowed to speak their own language in public — to do so meant expulsion to Siberia

186

— but they had managed through the years to speak it at home. In fact, the town authorities would never even admit there were Polish people living there.

Altogether I spent about three weeks in Zaslaw and having been fitted out with Russian-made garments I was able to walk around unnoticed in the daytime. I looked around the army barracks, which were mostly cavalry. I also got as near to the military aerodrome as I dared and tried to count the number of planes they had. Being a youngish boy, no one took a great deal of notice of me. I found that these planes were mostly bombers and in fact were some of those which had bombed Poland at the beginning of the war.

Another fascinating place I visited was the old Polish cemetery, dating back to the sixteenth century. I found many graves of generals, colonels and members of the aristocracy, as the Ukraine area of Russia belonged to Poland until the third partition in the eighteenth century.

I met a teacher, also of Polish ancestry, and she took me to her home and showed me a wonderful collection of books and magazines printed before the first world war. These books and magazines really surprised me as I had not known so many Polish families lived there in the past. Before the first world war, although it was Ukraine, they were permitted to lead their own political and social life [it was in fact part of the Russian Empire]. The Catholic churches organised them and kept the cultural life active as well as the faith. Before 1914 they were able to practice their own religion, print their own periodicals and in every way lead a free life. A great deal of land and property was owned by Polish noblemen until 1918, then after the Bolshevik revolution they were confiscated, and the owners sent to Siberia. This teacher told me that after the revolution, in order to intimidate the Polish families left in the area, the bodies of Polish priests were dug up from their graves and put on display — so as to prove that religion had finished and could not help the people in future.

The river Horyn also flowed through Zaslaw, and it had been dammed up to provide electricity for the town. It was a very picturesque place and in the past it had been a centre of culture and prosperity. At the time I was there, Joseph was overseeing the building of a large military installation, which Stalin had personally authorised. I saw the letters and documents signed by Stalin, authorising this work, which meant Joseph had priority to obtain many materials he required. An underground storage area had already been filled with large amounts of ammunition and other articles ready for later, as, according to Joseph's friends, Stalin planned to invade Germany once he had got Poland safely settled under his control. These plans were overtaken by Hitler when he invaded Russia in 1941.

Whilst at a family party, one of the officer's sons gave me a book about Lenin and the Spanish Civil War, which I believe saved my life.

During the interview, Viktor told me that there was a Russian officer at the party who played Russian roulette while he was there.

When I left Zaslaw for my return to Poland, I was able to walk in the daytime as I now wore my Russian-made clothing and was not at all conspicuous. I saw, for the first time, the enormous collective farms. The fields which had grown wheat in the summer had now been ploughed and I counted over one hundred tractors on one enormous piece of land alone; I was shocked to see that all the machinery used for threshing the corn had been left outside to rust. Apparently, no one bothered about State-owned property, and I saw far more government goods outside decaying through neglect. The houses where the collective farmers lived were also very neglected and looked as though they had never been painted. The workers were in rags — evidently there were shortages of every kind. I glanced in the window of one hardware shop and at least half of the shelves were stacked up with boxes of matches — and nothing else! But it would be possible to buy a million photographs of Lenin and Stalin, and every kind of propaganda magazine about the Soviet Union. Everywhere pictures of Lenin and Stalin were displayed, hanging amongst red flags. It grieved me to see such beautiful land neglected and I thought to myself, "What does Russia want with Poland when they have so much land of their own totally neglected?"

When approaching the border crossing, a civilian spotted me and instantly called the attention of the guards to me. Two guards arrested me, stuck their bayonets into my ribs and marched me into the guardroom. I was interrogated for several hours and told that if I did not tell the truth I would be shot as a spy. Their crossing rules state that it was ten years in prison for illegally crossing the border. The reason I gave for my visit to Russia was 1) that I had always been interested in Russia, having learned the language at school, and that as soon as I had the chance, I had decided to see it for myself, and 2) that I had a cousin in Zaslaw whom I wanted to see. The proof of my love for Russia was that I had a book about Lenin in my possession. They examined this book very thoroughly from cover to cover, obviously looking for secret writing between the lines. On finding nothing, they continued threatening me with a revolver, prepared a written statement and asked me to sign it, which I refused, and although terrified, I tried to pretend that it was all a joke. They left me overnight in a locked room with the window open, but with an Alsatian dog for company. Every time I moved — even a finger — the dog growled at me. I knew that if I jumped through the window I would be shot and I believe that is what they wanted me to do. The next morning, they opened the door and said, "You are free." They took me to the border and practically threw me across, and that was my very first visit to Stalinist Russia. My mother was simply furious when I arrived home, as she had spent anxious weeks wondering what I was up to.

By the middle of November 1939 Father returned home, in the middle of the night; we were shocked at his appearance. When the Polish army stopped fighting, he had escaped into the forest recovering any arms left around for future use and helping to create an underground resistance force. He was totally exhausted and very depressed that we had been unable to fight on two fronts. It would have been an enormous waste of manpower to continue fighting and so the Polish army had capitulated.

We were soon advised by friends that the newly set up occupation officials had a list of local people to be liquidated and they were making house-to-house searches day and night — looking for particular citizens — and anyone who they thought would oppose the new system. Our home was searched at least one a week, during the night, and each-time additional articles were taken away. As Father had previously been a member of the Czar's Guard he was on this list, and although he had successfully evaded detection so far, he decided to go back into the forests with several other officers, where they were organising an opposition group. In the meantime, I had to take food out *regularly and act as messenger for them. Many times I was followed by informers, most probably the Ukrainian minority group who were by then co-operating with the Russians, but I always managed to change my route and time of visits.*

When the weather deteriorated to a frost of minus 25centigrade my father had to return home, as it was impossible to sleep out for long under those conditions. Although the men had dug themselves a deep bunker, it was extremely cold and damp. Mother and I persuaded him to return home, if only for a short time, to recuperate and rest.

In the interview Viktor told me that his father was badly wounded in the leg.

Siberia

On 10ᵗʰ February 1940, a large posse of Russian troops encircled our home in the middle of the night. They broke down the front door with rifle butts and hammers and searched the house looking for Father. He had instantly run up into the attic, where he had a hand grenade and a revolver hidden but would not use it in case the whole family were arrested as a reprisal. Mother and my sister and I were made to stand in a corner of the room with our hands over our heads, still dressed in our nightclothes and trembling with fright. They found Father, dragged him downstairs, and told us to make up a small parcel with some clothes and enough food for one day and be ready to leave the house immediately.

We were put into a lorry and driven to the local railway station and locked into a cattle truck, with many other people from the town. Eventually there were so many of us that we could only stand up. The train stayed in the station for two weeks, without any sanitation or water. When we begged for water the KGB (NKVD) became very aggressive and told us we did not need water as we would die in any case. If anyone tried to escape, they were bayoneted to the ground — the men in charge saying that a bullet was too expensive to waste on us!

At the end of the two weeks, when the whole train was packed with many of the residents of Rovno who it was thought would oppose the system and who they wanted to eliminate, we started our journey towards Moscow. Just outside Moscow the train halted again, and we stayed there for six days, not knowing where we were being taken to. If we asked any of the guards, we were told we were going to the "land of the white bear"! We were occasionally given salted fish but no water. Wherever there was a small gap between the slats of the wagon, we put out our hands and caught snow, which then melted, and we drank it. The fish was so stale that we decided it was at least 20 years old; the taste was so repulsive that many people were immediately sick on tasting it. The very young children had no milk and could not eat the fish, so some of them died. Some of the elderly men, and anyone who became sick also died whilst the wagon was outside Moscow. It was extremely cold and the only way to sleep was to take it in turns to lie on the floor in between the legs of the people standing. The only way to keep up our spirits was to say prayers for our salvation, and then entertain ourselves by singing and telling stories — anything to occupy our minds. One or two of the wagon occupants completely lost their reason due to acute anxiety and depression.

After we left Moscow, the train headed east for Siberia, and from time to time the guards opened the truck, counted us and took away the dead. Imagine the sorrow of the families when a member of their family was taken away, not knowing whether they would be buried, or just thrown to the wolves. Eventually we came to the end of our journey — but even the railway guards had not got any orders as to what to do with us. By the time the instructions came through, a great many of our people were in a bad state of health and the guards gave us a little more food. I was so hungry that I felt I could have eaten a horse! I was desperately worried about my mother, as I thought I should have been able to help her more but there was nothing I could do.

When the instructions came through from the authorities, a lot of people came from collective farms with sledges and horses, and we were taken about fifty miles into the forest. It took several days to move the whole trainload. On our arrival we were settled into old barracks already full of Russian prisoners, who were overjoyed to see us, and immediately started to teach us all the tricks of survival.

In interview, Viktor said,

"When the communists started searching, they arrested Father. They arrest us and send us to Siberia. In the night, everybody and anybody who worked, they called us bloodsuckers. 'You are making the poor people in our country suffer so we have to eliminate you'. You could only take what you could carry. It was in winter — the coldest night of the year. If it was summer people might have survived, but in winter people die. Father was hidden in the attic. We had to learn German and Russian so I could understand them — it was important for us. They arrested us and took us to the station. All the families with children crying – all the chaos. Everyone was loaded into carriages used for animals – they were horrible. We were not fed for two weeks – no food. Only some people had something with them. We travelled two months to Siberia. From time to time the train would stop at a station and the dead would be carried off. So many people died on that journey. Then we had to establish ourselves there."

Because Father had been a high-ranking officer, they hated us. Our mother said, "Right this is your home, make yourselves comfortable."

We received about two square inches of bread each per day; the bread was not made with wheat, but with various kinds of poor-quality cereals; and nearly every day we had a bowl of fish soup – again made from salted fish – and very smelly. I made myself a peg to put on my nose so that I could eat this soup – otherwise I instantly vomited when I smelt it. The Russian prisoners advised us not to complain, saying, "You will soon get used to it and begin to like it!"

During the day we had to work in the forest, sawing down trees, clearing the bushes and building new barracks for the next arrival of prisoners. We were told that the Soviet Union had decided to remove the majority of people from the Russian-occupied part of Poland and take them to Siberia to work as slave labour and open up and develop the Siberian waste lands. Some of our original party had been directed to work in the mines. As more prisoners were brought in our group was moved on to clear further virgin forests, going east all the time. After many months of travelling, clearing forests and undergrowth, we were finally moved to an area so remote there were not even any barracks or huts for our sleeping accommodation. We had to cut down trees and build huts as our first priority.

The weather was intensely cold, and our clothes and shoes had begun to wear out. When we complained to our guards about the cold and lack of clothing, we were given old sacks to wrap our feet in and somehow make ourselves clothing. To protect our feet, we wrapped them in a sack, padded this with straw or moss, wrapped another layer of sack around it — put them in water to freeze solid and they held together for quite a time. The problem was that the sacking was thin, and we had to keep remaking the outer covering of the boots. They were so clumsy that we could only walk very slowly in them. Later on, we were given some old lorry tyres and we were able to make ourselves shoes from these. With a lot of improvisation, we were able to do this and with the rubber on the soles of our sacking shoes they were much stronger and kept our feet dry. We were lucky in having amongst us men who were really clever and able to make something out of nothing.

The guards had told us not to try to escape as even the wolves were starving in these forests. Our guards were from the Kalmyck and Mongolian regions, both oriental tribes, noted for their cruelty and indifference to human suffering. Our camp was near to the River Yenisei in the Putorana Mountains, but some of our people were sent as far east as the river Lena in eastern Siberia. We were still cutting trees, clearing the undergrowth and also breaking stones ready for roadmaking.

When we spent the winter in camp, the cold was frightening, the temperature could drop to -75 centigrade and this causes intense pressure on your heart and makes you feel very sleepy.

Even during the daytime, whilst working, you are only half-awake. The great danger is that if you sit down to rest and fall asleep, within ten minutes you could die from hypothermia. One person in each hut had to keep awake all through the night to build up the fire, otherwise if the fire went out every person in the hut would die. The men usually did this by rota.

Every morning, our first job was to take out the bodies of the people who had died during the night of weakness, dysentery, or general starvation. Some nights as many as 40 people died, mostly the very old or very young. We had to bury them, and during the winter the land was so frozen that we had, first of all, to light a fire to soften the ground and then afterwards we had to chop out the ground with choppers and bury them in very shallow graves. Even in the summer the ground thawed to only 6" in depth.

The seasons changed very quickly in Siberia. One day you had hard frost and the next day Spring came, the sun shone, the ground started to thaw and within a couple of day Spring flowers appeared.

Every night before we went to sleep, we held organised prayers and when the prayers started, the sobbing usually also began; and we called upon Almighty God to deliver us from this hell in which we found ourselves. This was a tremendous comfort for most of our people, and when thinking back I wondered how people survived without any faith to fall back on.

When Christmas came along, we all started to feel even more sorry for ourselves, and wondered what on earth we could find to provide some sort of food for our celebration of Christmas Eve — this night is celebrated in Poland with a feast which starts when the first star is sighted, and it is the main celebration of the Christmas period. After a meal consisting of twelve kinds of food (one for each apostle) the party usually finishes in tome for all to attend Midnight Mass. This Christmas, however, was certainly not going to be a cause for celebration. The Russians themselves totally ignore December 25th – their Orthodox religion held Christmas two weeks later than ours, and the Communists only had one day's holiday, namely 1st January, and this was really only an occasion to give gifts to the children. Their other main holidays were 8th March (Women's Day), 1st May (Labour Day) and 17th October when they celebrated the Revolution.

The children in the Camp School were the only ones allowed to have pens and paper, which were used to teach them the Russian language. They were able to draw Christmas cards for their parents and it looked as though this was going to be the only sign of Christmas. I worked all day on 24th December, and when returning to the barracks for the evening meal, I was told we were very lucky and there would be a very small piece of meat for everyone with the usual soup. I was shocked and wondered where this had come from. When we went for our meal, everyone received a tiny piece of well-roasted (almost burnt) very lean meat. I noticed that some had a piece of leg, and I became very puzzled as to what sort of animal we were eating. Some of the men jokingly said it was bear, as it was possible to kill them if you were really lucky, but it required several men and a lot of courage to catch and kill a bear. I knew it was not bear, as we would have had a larger portion each from such a large animal.

Anyway, we all ate our bit of meat and thoroughly enjoyed it. I was puzzled for quite a few days and finally I found the truth about the meat. I was horrified to find that the men had killed and cooked the camp guard's Alsatian watchdog — the one who kept guard on our own barracks. I knew the guard was looking for his dog, which had apparently wandered off whilst he was being exercised, and so I realised with horror that it was indeed this dog we had eaten with such relish. I could not believe that our people could be so cruel to such a beautiful animal. I knew we were starving and could eat anything, but my stomach turned over and I felt sick every time I thought about the dog. I was very sad to know that we had sunk so low as to kill and eat a dog. I told my friends. "In future, if you give me anything to eat it must not be dog." The guards must have been suspicious because they never again allowed the dogs to be let out for exercise unless accompanied by a guard, as they were very well trained and valuable animals.

A few days after Christmas I was called by the guards to clean their sleeping accommodation. My mother told me to keep my eyes open for anything I could get. Being young, I was able to get anywhere forbidden to adults and if anything could stick to my fingers or fit into my pockets it belonged to me! I cleaned their kitchen and found they had a lot of fish heads to be thrown on the rubbish tip- which was out of bounds to the prisoners. I filled my pockets with these fish heads and also inside my shirt and carried as many as I could back to Mother. On the way to the barracks, I was so hungry that I started to eat one of the fish heads in its raw state. I got through a large head but later began to be very sick because I could not digest the hard flesh. The next day I was so ill that I could not work and had to lie by the fire. Mother cooked all the fish heads, and with small bits of bread saved by other prisoners, she made an almost delicious fish soup.

One day there was a terrible row in the barracks, and we all rushed to see what was happening. The man who shared out the daily ration of bread had cut one piece lightly smaller than the rest and gave this smaller piece to one of the prisoners, who complained bitterly. There was a nasty argument, and eventually the prisoner went and fetched one of the choppers used in the forest and killed his opponent by striking him on the head. The guards came to see what had happened and only laughed, saying "Well, that's one capitalist less." We heard later that prisoners often killed for one slice of bread and the authorities never interfered in any arguments — but we were just told, "You must improve yourselves and become decent citizens and then you will be set free."

Another time there was a commotion in the guard's barracks, with a lot of shooting. A few days afterwards we were told that Russian prisoners had attacked the guards with the intention of stealing food and had killed several guards with their own weapons. In revenge the guards murdered about 30 Russian prisoners. Then we had to bury them. It was awful to see how badly they had treated their own people. We knew we were foreigners there and that we would be badly treated, but we never expected to see their own people being treated like animals.

The Commissar used to make unexpected visits to inspect the guards to see if they were maintaining control over the prisoners. On one such visit he arrived to find the guards all drunk. He was so bad tempered that he shot the guard's officer for dereliction of duty. We were shocked to see such terrible things happening to the Russian people and began to realise what justice really meant in Soviet Russia.

The guards were really brutal and after our people returned from interrogation, they were hardly recognisable from cuts and bruises. All the prisoners were interrogated in turn, as we were supposed to sign a statement admitting our faults and agreeing that we had seen our sentence. One of the prisoners about 40 years old, returned from his questioning with his eyes falling out of their sockets, and his whole-body red with blood. His arm and ribs had been broken as he had been knocked on the floor and jumped on by guards wearing heavy boots. After he refused to sign his paper, his eyes were gauged out of their sockets, and he was sent back to barracks to show us all what would happen if we refused to sign our statements. There was very little our people could do to help this man-only press cold snow on his bruises to help deaden the pain. He begged us to kill him as he could not bear the pain any longer. He died two days later, and we had to bury him.

This interrogation went on daily by a political commissar until everyone in the camp had been interviewed, mock evidence prepared, and a sentence prescribed. We were usually called into the guard's room at about 2:00 am, stripped naked and strapped to a table, with the various forms of abuse clearly visible in the room. If the prisoner refused to sign the statement immediately, icy water was thrown over him and then two men with rubber truncheons were ready to beat him until unconscious. This was standard treatment for men and women alike. It was particularly humiliating for the women in the camp and when anyone returned from such treatment, we were all waiting to try to help them in any way we could, either with their cuts and bruises, or just to cheer them up as much as we could after their ordeal. No-one ever thought it would be possible to escape alive from this hell on earth.

When it was my turn to be interrogated my report said that I had fought against the Communists in the first World War. When I told them politely that I had not been born until 1925, I was beaten and told "No-one asked when you were born. We are telling you to sign and then we will leave you alone." [At the last interview with Viktor in 2020, Mary told me that they now thought he had been born in 1923 because a distant relative had told them so.] *It was written on this report that I freely agreed that what was written above was correct, and I also agreed to be held in prison for ten years.*

To our great shock the Commissar knew Father's whole history, even back to his education in St Petersburg. My father refused to sign his confession and finally, after being severely beaten, he was shot personally by the Commissar. We were not allowed to see his body and never knew whether he was buried or thrown out for the wolves to eat. I cannot bear to think about it even after 50 years. We later realised, that if my father had not been shot in the camp, he would have been shot with the thousands of Polish officers murdered in the forest at Katyn in Russia.

In interview Viktor told me:

"They bring us some horrible food. There were kids screaming, ladies crying, but what can you do? We settled down and found jobs like cutting trees. We had only one axe – two boys with ten trees to cut – otherwise you would have nothing to eat. They would come with one potato and then say, "You haven't cut enough – no food for you today." So, we had to work terribly hard to earn the food. Eventually, I decided to escape.

There was an interrogation about Father. There was a big table — one Russian political officer sitting at the table and Father on the other side. They were asking, "You have been serving Tsarist king — you are enemy of the state — the working-class people suffer — you persecute them." Then Father said something which the Russian didn't like and bang — and the blood — you should have seen his head — blood terrible — I screamed and fell down. It was so upsetting to see my own father there. Because I was by my father they said, "Get off or we'll shoot you as well." I fell on my father and covered him — somehow his legs were still moving although he had died. [Mary explained that in the account she had recorded in 1995 Viktor had not wanted to repeat the details of his father's death and so had said that he wasn't there.]

Mother was shouting and crying — but nothing you can do — people ran and told Mother, "Your husband has been shot." Terrible lamenting and all the usual procedure. I put my arm around my mother and said, "I will look after you — they won't kill you."

How many times they broke my nose? How many times they kick me and treat me like an animal? I soiled myself under interrogation. You ask yourself, 'Why don't you shoot me?' You wish you were dead. They even try to be nice and offer you nice food and then beat you again. I didn't know what my father had done. [Mary told me that Viktor still has nightmares about it.]

My sister was a very clever girl. They wanted to change all children for the communist education — propaganda for the children, "You don't want to be a capitalist." So, she was so clever — my sister — she had a photographic memory. I was jealous. In school I had to learn — to memorise — but she was so clever. They decided to take children away to Moscow — them who they wanted. And they took my sister — Mother didn't want to let her go — she was crying and everything else. Because she was so clever, she became a medical student, and she was educated a year or two. There were terrible shortages because of the war. She got tuberculosis. Because she had TB, they let her come to see the camp. She packed some things and she come back to see us in the camp, but she was dying — because Russia hadn't got any medicine. She stayed only three days and we hoped she got back safely. We never saw her again — she died. So, Mother and me survived." [Viktor did not say when she died — this may have been much later, long after the war.]

Following my father's death in the early Spring, I decided to try to escape. I knew it would be a long and dangerous journey and that I may not survive, but it was better than to stay where I was. Mother encouraged me to do this, as she thought if I escaped at least one member of the family would survive. Some of the older men also encouraged us boys to go. They taught us all they knew about survival and what to eat, how to sleep safely on the journey and also how to cross the rivers. I had already learned most of this from my Scouting days in Poland, but every little bit of encouragement helped.

We prepared for my escape by saving half of my daily bread ration and drying it. I also made myself a knife from the metal rings from a wooden barrel which had contained dried fish. I secretly spent many hours sharpening this piece of metal because we were not allowed to have any sharp tools in case we attacked the guards.

The guards were sometimes quite friendly with us when they were drunk, and during their drunken bouts, we were able to complete our arrangements. From time to time, the camp guards had to fetch supplies form another base and needed prisoners to help load up the trucks. When we were ready to go, my friend Tomasz and I volunteered to help, and when we got to the point where we had to load the supplies, our guards got drunk, and we were able to steal some bread and make our escape. If I had known what a terrible time we were to have I would never have attempted the journey. Our aim was to go towards the Caspian Sea. We did not have a compass but used the sun and the moss on trees to point out our direction.

In interview Viktor told me:

"I escaped. Why? Because I said to everybody, "I want to go back – I have to fight – I have to fight for my father." My father was everything for me, because our family was very close. So therefore, I decided to go. Everybody in the camp said, "You will never get there. What? You are just a kid! What about the wolves? The police? You have no food – what can you eat? There will be nothing to eat except berries." There were a lot of berries there and the birds lived on the berries.

There was a Russian prisoner who told us about the berries. Mother asked, "How could he survive?" and the Russian said. "He can – he can eat berries."

But wolves, wolves — in the night — howling — that was enough to frighten you. But I said, "No, my father, I will fight the Russians because of my father." My mother didn't want me to go. Everybody said, "Don't go — you'll never see him again — it's impossible — what are you going to eat? Where are you going to sleep? It's thousands of miles to Iran [it is possible that he meant Iraq — that is where the British army were at that time]. I go by Lake Baikal, have a look some time on a map where it says Lake Baikal; I pass by that. But I already knew Russian geography because my father wanted to educate me. I decided to go. Mother said, "Look, what can I do? I can't hold him — he might die here — he might just as well die on the way." So, we said goodbye to all the people. They said, "You are a kid; you don't know what you are doing; you have no sense; just talk to him." But I said, "Nobody can tell me what to do. I am going to fight because I want to fight for my father," So I decided to go. Everybody said goodbye, and ladies crying. Everybody gave me a little bit — and that's it. I made myself a weapon; there was a metal ring around the bottles that came with food in and I kept it. I cut it — it took days — and sharpened it and put a piece of wood and tied it to that. If the wolves attack me, I have something to fight with. They asked me where I am going to sleep, and I answered anywhere I can. I didn't go in the daytime; I went in the night because I didn't say goodbye to Mother because of the tears."

The worst obstacles were the many very wide fast-flowing Siberian rivers we had to cross, and also the vast expanses of uninhabited terrain we had to cover. We eat anything we could find, and our main source of food was berries from the huge variety of bushes growing on the Siberian plains and in the forests. I had been told in the camp that if a bird eats berries from a bush or tree, they would be safe for humans to eat; so we followed this advice and when we came across a bush, we stripped all the berries off and carried as many as we could, to last until we found more. We had a lot of trouble with diarrhoea as we had nothing solid or warm to eat, and we had a great deal of stomach-ache. Some of the berries were bitter but if there was nothing else, we had to eat them.

We started to lose our energy and got very depressed and thin. We walked on during the daylight hours and slept up on the branches of trees at night, because of the wolves roaming the area. We could hear their terrifying howls from a distance. At one stage the wolves found our scent and followed us to the base of our tree. They stayed there for three days, and we had to stay on the branches of the tree without food until they got tired of waiting and ran off. To be safe, we always tied ourselves to the branches of the tree so that we would not fall off in our sleep. When we had to cross a river, we built a raft each from bundles of twigs. We needed a huge amount of small branches and twigs to take our weight, and then we had to twist small twigs until we could make a sort of rope to tie the bundle together. We then took off all our clothes, tied them to the back of our necks, and set off paddling the rafts with our hands and pushing ourselves to the other side of the river. It usually took about a mile's length of the river before you could get to the opposite bank, as Siberian rivers are very fast flowing. When we reached the other side, our hands were blue with cold and very stiff. We had to dress ourselves and runs as fast as our strength would allow to warm our hands and bodies and get our circulation going.

After a few weeks' travelling in this way my friend became ill, I think with pneumonia, and early one morning he collapsed and died. I was very upset and depressed because we had got on very well together and I felt I had lost a true friend. I scratched a hole in the ground with sticks, buried him and covered the mound with stones, and sadly moved on.

In interview Viktor told me:

"Then I walked and walked. [In the interview Viktor made no mention of his friend Tomasz] But the wolves; they told me if you hear wolves from the distance, look for a tree. Look for a tree because they will come for you; they are hungry. They chase deer, anything to eat, masses of wolves. So, I thought I will fight by the tree but if I hear from a distance, I'll go up a tree; I can hear them howling, so I know wolves are near. So, I looked for a tree you can climb. But I have cold hands. I am frightened; it's not so easy. So, I heard wolves and I could hear them getting nearer and nearer, so off I go to find a tree. First one will come to lead them; and after the first one all the wolves come together; they can smell; they know I am there; they want to get me. Then they start jumping on the tree and claw the bark; they pull off all the bark to try to get me. It was so terrifying. I told myself "Be brave; you chose that way."

The wolves went away but I didn't go straight away; wait till they have gone, then get down and walk and look for the parts where there are little berries growing.

When it is open land – no trees there – the berries grow; the berries are for the birds, that's why the birds live there. So, I collected everything I could and put it in my shirt – everywhere I could. Three times I was attacked by wolves at least. The noise they make to get me down out of the trees; terrific; frightening; more frightening than anything, and when they go away, don't go straight away; see if they go and then just carry on. But determination; without determination I wouldn't have gone on."

From then on, I became very doubtful that I would survive and I got even more depressed and stopped washing myself. Every day when I got tired, I decided that it would be better to finish myself off, and whenever I sat by a river contemplating the best place to cross over, a voice inside my head told me to jump into the lovely clear water and that would bring me peace – why bother to struggle on as you will fail in any case. But another voice answered, "Do it tomorrow, as that will be better than doing it today – just see what tomorrow brings." That happened to me on very many occasions. From then on, I decided that for all my future life I would always leave difficult decisions until tomorrow.

Many parts of Siberia have perma-frost; in the Summer this slightly thaws and creates bogs, and on this bogland millions and millions of mosquitoes breed; so many that the sky can appear black with them. They are an appalling nuisance to people and to animals, and the only way to protect yourself is to cover as much of your body as possible. They get into your eyes, mouth and hair looking for blood and it has been known for mosquitoes to bite a horse to death, and also reindeers. The reindeers run into the bushes to drive the insects away. When I was resting, I used to light a fire and sit as near to it as possible. If I was lucky enough to find pine branches, I would build the fire up with these and create a lot of smoke — this was the best way I could find to deal with them. If the ground was very wet or if I could not find dry wood to light a fire, I would cover my face, hands and feet with a thick layer of mud; when this dried it was difficult for the insects to bite. I covered many miles plastered with mud but fortunately, never met anyone in these areas of bogland.

I was very relieved when I reached the inhabited part of Siberia where I started to see people and small settlements and felt I may have a chance of survival. As I travelled on, I met many different tribes who did not understand the Russian language. I was now able to find more food — one elderly shepherd I met gave me some of his meal consisting of boiled lamb; that nearly killed me, as it was very greasy, and my stomach was not used to meat or rich food. It was my fault for eating too much, but I was absolutely starving and had not had anything warm to eat for many months.

On another occasion I saw a few houses and went to beg for food. The people were very suspicious of me, locking me in a shed whilst they decided what to do with me. They thought I was a KGB [NKVD] spy. I had a great deal of difficulty in persuading them that I was far too young to be a spy and that I was an escaped prisoner from the camps. Fortunately, they believed me and gave me food and shelter for a few weeks until I regained my strength. In repayment for their kindness, I chopped all the wood for the families enough to last them for several months.

Most of these people had a lot of meat from the animals in the forest which they dried and stored for the winter months, but they were extremely short of bread and other foodstuffs. They lived a very primitive life; their clothes and shoes were made from animal skins; they had no beds but slept on furs and moss on wooden slats. I very often thought they were themselves hiding from the Communist oppression and that is why they were so helpful to me after establishing that I was no danger to them. I walked as far as I could every day, without worrying how many miles I travelled, because my main priority was always finding food. Sooner or later, something turned up, but I always thought that it would be impossible to feel completely full. My only dream was to have a really delicious hot meal and then lie down and die!

In interview Viktor told me:

"I walked for days and days getting tired. I don't know how long because you lose sense – you lose everything else. It took all my determination to go."

On one occasion I saw some men tending cattle and horses and crept towards them to see what they were doing and who they were. As I watched I was grabbed from behind by two men, who thought I was after their animals. They dragged me to their hut and questioned me in a language half Russian and the other half a language unknown to me, accusing me of wanting to steal their animals as evidently this had previously happened to them. They tied my legs together so that I could not escape, and I had great difficulty in making them understand that I did not want their animals. After several hours of questions, I managed to make them understand that I was Polish and was trying to get to the Caspian Sea and I had to point out to them in which direction it lay. After some arguments between them, the eldest man gave me something to eat. At first, they sat eating in front of me, making my mouth water excessively. When I grabbed a bone, they had finished with and started to gnaw it, they took it from me, gave it to the dogs and gave me some food. They decided to feed me because I had not tried to escape — they reasoned that if I had tried to escape it would prove I was trying to steal one of their animals.

They decided to let me stay with them as one of their workers. I had to tend the fire and look after the cooking pot, which was suspended over the fire. I spent most of the time chopping wood and I also had to comb their hair every night to remove head lice. Another job was to boil their clothes to kill the fleas. To my horror they had only one pot, and when not being used to wash clothes in, was also used to cook the food. Nevertheless, the food was wonderful and soon restored my strength, but being rich and greasy it upset my stomach until I had got acclimatised to it. Until then, I had started to lose my vison and my teeth had gone soft through lack of vitamins and food. All my bones stuck out and I could count every rib. I was just skin and bones. At this stage, the voice inside my head stopped telling me to kill myself and I began to feel more cheerful.

My captors were still quite suspicious of me, and tied my legs together every night, thinking I might kill them in their sleep and make my escape. When I felt stronger, I started to plead with them to let me continue on my journey, but they always refused as by now I was very useful to them. Finally, I told them I would stay with them always; they were very pleased, and we started to build a new hut for me. I made some suggestions to improve their huts so that they would be more comfortable and also showed them how to build a place to smoke their meat.

One of their men fell ill and they were so concerned that they lost interest in me. This was the opportunity I had been waiting for and early one morning, when they were milking the cattle, I slipped away. As I had previously told them the direction of the Caspian Sea and that I was going that way, I went off in the opposite direction in case they came after me. This was a long diversion to take but I thought it would be safer.

I carried on with my journey but lost my way because the weather was very cloudy for a few days, and I was unable to decide which was North and which was South – I was following a Southwestern direction, so I lay low until the weather changed. Whilst walking along another time I heard dogs barking in the distance, so I made my way in that direction. When I got closer, I also heard a cock crowing so I knew I was near to habitation and soon came across a few houses. Again, I was met with suspicion, but the people here understood Russian, so we were able to talk easily together. As usual I was asked "Who are you? And where are you going?" and so on. I had to give a good explanation as the men carried hunting weapons and knives. After telling them why I was here and where I had come from the men permitted me to stay with them for some time to regain my strength. Although they were of Eastern origin, we knew enough Russian to be able to talk together. They knew what was happening in the world and to my great shock I heard that Germany had attacked Russia and that heavy fighting was taking place. Imagine my joy in hearing *that Russia was receiving some of the medicine they had doled out to Poland!*

Following this news, I had to decide whether to try to get back to Poland or whether to continue my original intention to leave Russia via Persia. Eventually I thought it would be quite impossible to get through a battle area so decided to continue with my journey to the Caspian Sea. I still had a long distance to cover and hoped I had at least reached halfway.

In interview Viktor told me:

"So many things happened to me on the journey. When I went further south something important happened to me. I heard some dogs barking. The land there was occupied by people who live in tents. I had hallucinations and imagined all sorts of things – I imagined Mother calling me. I heard the dog barking and I thought am I imagining? I don't know how long I had been walking because it is quite a distance from Siberia to the south. You pray every night and every day. There is no one else to help you, only Almighty God will help you – nothing else matters."

I started having hallucinations, possibly through physical exhaustion, lack of proper food and anxiety. Again, I had severe doubts that I would survive – I started to hear music quite clearly – sounding like the large military orchestras I had heard at home. I heard my mother's voice telling me what to do, and I even imagined I was back at school, working on a project, or that I was with my friends in the Boy Scouts preparing to go on camp. I also quite clearly saw cathedrals and large churches in the distance. I always had these vision

213

in the evening — sometimes they were pleasant and at other times absolutely terrifying. I saw the tragedy of war flashing before my eyes, the bloodshed and everything horrible it was possible to imagine. As quickly as these hallucinations came, they suddenly vanished, and I became confused as to whether I had really seen something or imagined it.

I was now passing through farmland and pastures, the weather was warm, and I was able to find more food, either from the fields or given to me by kindly people. Mobilisation was taking place now and shortages had increased. I was occasionally able to talk to people on the road and they told me of the various rumours persisting all over the country. The Government had withdrawn information about the war from the general public; people had been told to double their efforts and work together to fight the Germans, but the majority of people had to rely on rumours to know what the state of the war was.

People were still suspicious of me — looking so ragged and skinny — but the fact that I was a youngster saved me from being taken for a spy. Whenever I stayed anywhere for good, I was usually told by the village elder to leave as quickly as possible or they may get into trouble for helping a stranger. I always skirted around the larger villages, to avoid the possibility of being picked up by either police or military personnel. It was often 50 to 100 miles between villages, and I kept thinking I would never come to the end of it all.

Sometimes I saw a train, far from habitation, just standing on the railway lines in the middle of a field. I did no know why they were there or for how long they were going to stay. Twice I did hitch lifts on trains. Once I went in the wrong direction and it took me several days to regain lost ground, but the second time it was very successful and I managed to ride in a goods train for about 300-400 miles, as close as I could guess.

Many times I was able to hitch a lift on a goods lorry, but the drivers usually expected a tip, and when I told them I had no money I was often dumped quickly. I never gave up trying, as this was my last hope to cover longer distances than by walking. I was getting very fond of the native people and hoped that the Germans would be able to destroy the Communist system. The Russians themselves seemed nervous and suspicious of everyone; they had no freedom and could not dare to criticise authority — in fact the whole country was more or less a giant prison camp. They were terrified to discuss their conditions in case they were overheard and denounced as a traitor — that meant either instant elimination or imprisonment in Siberia — and very often they perished there.

Two kindly elderly gentlemen fishing in a small lake helped me for a few days. They hid me in their hut and for the very first time I had a meal of fresh fish — it was wonderful — together with a form of flat barley bread, something like chapatis, which they baked over an open fire. I had truthfully not enjoyed such food since I left home, despite the bread being covered in dust from the fire I ate every single crumb. The fishermen wanted me to stay with them, as they had a government quota saying they must produce a certain amount of fish every day for a local store and they were finding it difficult to fulfil this. I explained to them that I could not stay.

I left the lake and walked through miles and miles of pastureland until I came upon a tented community, with the men tending cattle, horses, and sheep in the fields around. They took me in, and, for the first time, I had as much food as I wanted. From experience I knew I had to start with small meals, as my stomach could not manage to take as much as I thought I could eat. I still suffered acute stomach pain, and one day, grovelling on the ground in agony I had managed to push out a small hole in the soil. When the women saw I was ill they prepared some medicine for me which one of the men forced me to take. It was horrible, and I remember the taste to this day over 50 years later. I found out afterwards that it was made from horses' urine.

After recovering from this severe stomach trouble, they told me I had to work for the food I had eaten and I was treated like an animal, or a prehistoric man, because of my appearance. I was still dressed in sacking and my hair was long and unkempt. They told me they would 'civilise' me and I was kept a distance from the families and children in case I passed any disease on to them. Only the dogs were friendly with me, and, in fact, I slept with the dogs on skins out-of-doors.

Everyone in this small community had to work. The women dyed wool and wove the most beautiful carpets, with which the children also helped. Some of the carpets were hung around the walls of their tents and the colours were rich and vibrant. They sold other carpets to bring in additional income. As I began to feel fitter and more cheerful, I was able to tell them how I came to be there. They could hardly believe that I had survived such an ordeal. They found me some old clothes and set me to work tending the cattle and sheep. After some time, they decided amongst themselves that I would be useful to them and that I would be old enough to marry one of their daughters. They started preparing for the wedding. I knew nothing of this because the majority of their conversation was in their own tongue which I could not understand. One of the young girls started smiling at me and I wondered why, as previously no one ever came very close to me. One day, one of the men told me that she would be my bride, but that I had first to prove myself by carrying out some tasks on horseback, as this was the traditional way to win the bride.

I viewed the prospect with horror and told him that I had no intention of getting married and that I was not old enough in any case. He told me I was quite old enough according to their custom, but, in any case, if I did not really like her, I could easily divorce her later. I immediately started to plan my departure from this group, but with some disappointment, as I dreaded going back to not knowing where my next meal was coming from. If they had not been planning a wedding, I would have stayed there for several months.

A couple of days later, on returning from the fields, I heard the sound of singing accompanied by drumming. When I asked what was happening, I was told there would be three days of celebration, at the end of which I would perform the task on horseback and, if successful, the bride would accept me. A tent had been prepared for us and I was shown the clothes I would wear for the ceremony and the strange hat to match. I was then told that I would work several years for my father-in-law to pay for his daughter. I started to shake with fright.

In the evening I was shown the new tent and told I would now be able to sleep there with the bride, but with a carpet rolled up in between us to prevent me touching her — this was just to get used to each other. My bride-to-be started to take liberties with me, she patted me and smiled very sweetly

— *imagine my horror and the urgency of my need to make a hasty departure. Early next morning, I ate as much food as I possibly could, and hid as much cooked meat around my body as I could manage — mostly horsemeat. When I was given my chores for the day, I went off as though going to work and then ran off as quickly as I could. One of the dogs had taken a liking to me and used to spend the day with me at work. He was a problem now as he continued to follow me, barking all the time when I tried to send him back. I did not know what to do and even contemplated killing him, but eventually he got the message and went back to the living quarters.*

In interview Viktor told me:

"The people, who lived only in tents, and had animals in the pasture, they saw me and were terrified of me. I was terrible, scratched and could only walk with a stick. They gave me something to eat and I stayed there for about a week or maybe two. I get to like them, but they couldn't speak Russian because they were a different people. After I got used to them, I explained who I am — all the stories — and they said, 'Well stay with us.' But I didn't want to stay with them — I wanted to go.

One day — I had been with them on the fields with the boys — we come back from the fields, and I heard music playing. I said, 'What is that?' They said, 'There will be a wedding.' I said, 'Who is the lady?' they said, 'That girl — with a long skirt down to the floor.' And I said, 'Who is she going to marry?' They said, 'You.' I said, 'What? You must be joking.' I said, 'How can that be?' and they said, 'There are no men here. We are short of men – she needs to get married.' I didn't believe them – I thought they were joking.

The next day when we came back, they showed me beds made on the floor in the tent and said that will be your place. I said, 'My place?' and they said, 'And that's for your wife – your bride.' They all started dancing and there was music and food. It was horrible – I thought this is rubbish. I went to go to sleep, and she was lying by me. She kept putting her arm around me and I said go away. I got up and went outside and ran away into the trees. I told myself this is not my wife – I don't think about wives. They said don't worry he will come back.

I decided in the night – I go. So I got up very early and hid myself in the bushes but they sent the dog after me and they were shouting and calling for me. They found me and said, 'What are you doing here?' I said, 'Looking for something – I don't know.' So I went back and they were all laughing at me. I told myself – that's enough, I'm ready to go. One day I decided – we were looking after the animals, and they were usually losing animals, and somebody had to go and find them with the dogs. I pretended that I was going to look after the animals and hid in the bushes. I could hear them shouting but this time they lost me. That's how I got away."

Travelling was much easier after that, for one thing I had some fairly respectable clothing and my hair had been cut and I had a few days' supply of cooked meat. As I was getting closer to the Caspian Sea, the terrain was flat and below sea level and the weather becoming very warm and pleasant.

While resting besides a river a short way from a village and collective farm, I heard a lot of laughter and a large crowd of girls ran out from the farm buildings towards the river, obviously for a swim during their break. To my dismay they all stripped off and jumped naked into the river, swimming and splashing around playfully. Seeing me, they decided that I should join them. I was far too shy to swim with a crowd of naked women and said I could not swim. They howled with laughter at my apparent shyness, and dragged me into the water still clothed, washing my face and hair for me with their soap, having decided I needed a good clean up. Afterwards they combed my hair into some order and one of the ladies, a rather pleasant middle-aged woman, said she had room in her house for me, as her husband was away at the war, and she had a lot of odd jobs needing attention. I was not very keen to go with her, but the crowd of girls persuaded me as I should have some food and rest, otherwise I might die from starvation. They were very kind to me in a motherly way and I stayed in the village for some weeks.

I worked for my 'landlady' in her garden, mending the fence, repairing her garden tools, painting the inside of the house with lime-wash and finally, repairing her stone-built fireplace which had already half collapsed. Her neighbours were all very interested, thinking I was very practical and innovative and many of them wanted me to do odd jobs for them. It was soon obvious that the village consisted of women, children and very old men and they all seemed to work on the collective farm. It was impossible for them to get any help from anyone and so I was quite useful to them, in return for my board and lodgings.

The ladies came to me for all sorts of advice — one desperate woman came to ask if I could look after her baby because she was ill and no one knew what was wrong. It did not matter how much I tried to impress upon her that I was not a doctor or nurse and knew nothing about illness, she told me, "You know more than I do, and you might be able to help." Another time I had to repair a wooden leg for an elderly man. I took the stump and inserted into it a fresh bit of wood where it had broken, and it was wearable again. By this time, the manager of the collective farm had heard about me and took me to visit the farm. He only had female labour and needed another male to help with the work women were not used to carrying out. For him I repaired a milk church and a tractor. I had never had anything to do with a tractor before, but I cleaned it and tightened up all the loose screws and bolts and to my relief it was able to start up. The manager suggested to me that he would get me a set of official papers and register me as a farm worker. I agreed temporarily, as I always took every opportunity to earn my food and rebuild my strength.

When I felt strong and fitter, I told Tanya, whose house I was staying in, that I was to continue my journey shortly. She wanted to come with me as she said the manager at the factory was abusing her and the other girls and she would like to move further south. I advised her that even if she moved, she would still have to work hard, and she might not even get such good accommodation and work as she had here. After collecting a stock of food, gathering together a better-looking outfit and cutting my hair, I started to look far more human and started off more cheerfully.

By now the Summer was really hot and I was able to sleep in haystacks and other such places. It was warm enough to sleep outdoors without any discomfort. After one such really good night's sleep inside a haystack, I had slept longer than usual and heard a swishing noise not too far away from me. I raised my head and peered through the hay, and, at the same moment an old lady who was collecting the hay and making the noise, saw me and screamed with fright. She raised her arms and ran shouting that she had seen a ghost. After running about 100 yards, she stopped and turned around to see what was inside the stack; I crawled out and called to her not to be frightened, but she would not come near me.

Another time, I was walking through a large area of country growing only watermelons. As there was no other food about, I picked a large melon and thoroughly enjoyed biting into the juicy fruit. After continuing for many miles with only melons for food, I started to have severe diarrhoea and was in such trouble that the only way to preserve my clean clothes was to walk without my trousers on, as I had to relieve myself so frequently that I had not got time to take them off. I also had to clean myself up in a river later. Hygiene is most important when living off the land, especially in hot weather. As usual, my first priority was finding food. I never had any choice about what to eat — I just had to eat what was available at the time. Any farm produce along the road automatically belonged to me and I always said a grateful prayer to the people who planted it.

Of course, many other things happened which are not included in this chapter, for instance I have not mentioned the marvellous scenery and incredible vastness of Siberia; the beautiful and varied wildflowers, the midnight sun, the enormous flocks of birds migrating in the Spring to their nesting sites in warmer climes, nor the very small mammals I saw on the way and the enormous herds of reindeer. The rivers in themselves were absolutely wonderful, and wider than any seen in Europe. But I was not there to enjoy nature — my only aim was to survive. The only birds I was absolutely overjoyed to see were the first few seagulls which told me that at last I was approaching the Caspian Sea.

On my way towards the Caspian Sea, I had to cross great marshes and the country became heavily populated. I had to be very careful not to get too close to the KGB (NKVD) or military personnel. By now, the country was on full war alert, and I saw tremendous movements of army vehicles, which cheered me up as I hoped Poland would be liberated. I was generally ignored by ordinary civilians, as I was again looking like a scarecrow with my ragged clothing and skeleton-like appearance. I did not worry how I looked — I only worried about food. I began to think what I would do if ever I could get back to Rovno and had made up my mind to organise a gang of people to carry on with sabotage on a large scale. I also wanted everyone to know that Siberia consisted mainly of concentration camps, not only holding thousands of Polish people, but also thousands of Russians (including many Orthodox priests) who had criticised the system, besides the remnants of wealthy people whose lands they had confiscated during the years of revolution.

When I finally arrived at a small fishing village on the coast, I got talking to an old gentleman who I think came from Georgia; he told me that many people were already escaping to the West, namely Persia, and the best way to get there was on a small fishing craft, but you had to pay for the journey. As I had no money at all this created a major problem, so he invited me to go home with him whilst looking around to see what could be done. I gladly accepted this offer. He himself hated the Government of Russia and told me to pray and wait for better times. In his opinion Russia was going to be punished for their crimes against humanity.

I worked in his garden removing weeds, feeding the chickens, and doing any other odd jobs that needed attention. At the same time, with his help, trying to find a way round my problem – although he suggested I should stay with him permanently. I told him I had travelled so far and was not going to give up at this stage. He had friends in another village and took me along to meet them, hoping they might take me out fishing with them and drop me off somewhere along the Persian coast. Unfortunately, no one wanted to do this, because if caught, they would be severely punished and could possibly even end up in Siberia themselves, as this would be regarded as a crime against the Sate. They did suggest, however, that I moved to another small port a little further along the coast where boats took passengers to Persia (Iran).

This I did and finding an empty boat, got on it and hid under a large pile of nets and went to sleep. No one came to this boat for several days, so I reluctantly decided to try elsewhere. During the daytime I watched the movement of other boats in this port but returned to my hiding place under the fishing nets to sleep at night. Again, I approached an old gentleman hanging around the port (the young people were never helpful) and told him of my predicament. He questioned me as to who I was, and I said I was a Muslim trying to get into Persia. He was not at all convinced until I told him I had come from the Tartar settlement who lived in Poland, and that this minority group had remained in Poland to this day, even having their own mosques. This finally decided him to help me. He gave me advice on condition that I did not disclose I had received any information from him as to how to get into Persia. I willingly agreed to this as I knew it would be regarded as treason on his part if he helped me to escape from Russia.

He told me to go to a village further along the coast where I would find larger boats, travelling regularly to Persia, carrying passengers and goods. I still did not know how to get on a boat as there was always someone standing at the bottom of the gangway checking passengers on. However, I saw porters carrying boxes and goods on board and making several journeys on and off the boat without being watched. I went along and helped them. No one gave me a second glance as I climbed aboard carrying a large box. I then found myself a good hiding place and waited for the boat to set sail.

After arrival in Persia, I did not even know the name of the village or port where we landed, I joined the gang of people unloading the boat and got off unnoticed. But on leaving the area where the goods were unloaded, I had to go through a control point, and I was picked up by the guard as I had no papers. They wanted to put me back on the boat, but in desperation I screamed and shouted that I did not want to go back and that I was not Russian. I was then passed over to *another official and he interrogated me in Russian as to who I was, where I had come from and where I wanted to go.*

Only my persistence persuaded them I was Polish, and they took me into an office block and locked me in one of the offices. Evidently, they forgot all about me. I was grateful at first and slept on the floor during the night. By next morning I desperately wished to use a toilet, so I started banging on the door and walls of the office hoping someone would hear me. Finally, a man came and opened the door and was astonished at my appearance. I told him I had been locked in all night and needed to use the toilet. At first, he did not know what to do with me, but seeing my miserable state he arranged for me to be admitted to the local hospital, where I was given pyjamas, and someone washed and fed me. After at least two weeks in hospital, another group of people came into the ward, and I heard them speaking in Polish. I then realised that there were other Polish people in this area and found out that these men were prisoners being repatriated from Russia to join a Polish army being organised to help fight against the Germans. This was my salvation.

Looking back on my journey I felt most relieved that I did not have to kill anything in order to survive. The only flesh I had found for myself were the meat from a dead reindeer and a dead crow. All in all, my escape had taken just under twelve months; there was no accurate way of recording the mileage of my journey, but I must have covered between 4,000 – 5,000 miles.

rock a
water p